ESSENTIAL

HYDRAULICS
AND
HYDROLOGY

HAESTAD
PRESS

**HAESTAD
PRESS**

Essential Hydraulics and Hydrology

Copyright ©1998 Haestad Methods, Inc.
All Rights Reserved.

Haestad Methods, Inc. trademarks
The following are registered trademarks of Haestad Methods, Inc:
CADMAGIC, CulvertMaster, Cybernet, FlowMaster, StormCAD, WaterCAD.

The following are trademarks of Haestad Methods, Inc:
HECPack, POND-2, Pond Pack, SewerCAD, Graphical HEC-1, Graphical HEC-Pack.

Haestad Methods is a registered tradename of Haestad Methods, Inc.
Haestad Press is a registered tradename of Haestad Methods, Inc.

All other brands, company or product names or trademarks belong to their respective holders.

ISBN Number 0-9657580-5-2
LCCN 98-88726

Contributing Editors

Benjamin Ewing

Michael K. Glazner

Walter M. Grayman, Ph.D., PE

Jeremy Haynes

Gregg A. Herrin

Darrow Kirkpatrick

Kelly L'Heureux

Sasa Tomic, Ph.D.

Thomas Walski, Ph.D., PE

Benjamin White

Benjamin Wilson

Editor in Chief

Adam M. Strafaci

Peer Review

Donald V. Chase, Ph.D., PE

University of Dayton

Michael Meadows, Ph.D., PE

University of South Carolina

To our mentors

Contents

SECTION IV Business and Computers 133

Preface

Haestad Press evolved out of what the engineers at Haestad Methods saw as the necessity for affordable, quality reference and textbooks dedicated to the practical application of engineering theory to hydraulics and hydrology. In civil engineering education, scientific methods tend to be emphasized over practical and technological approaches to problem-solving, creating a gap between theoretical knowledge and the ability to apply that knowledge in real-world situations. This presents a serious problem, especially in the area of hydraulics and hydrology since the entire world depends on civil engineers every day for safe drinking water, reliable sewer systems and protection from floods.

Haestad Methods has long recognized this problem which consequently divides our interests. As a software company, we are committed to the development of quality computer applications and technical support that provide civil engineers with effective and efficient solutions for complex engineering design, analysis and modeling tasks. On the other hand, because of the lack of resources addressing the practical application of technical knowledge, we also feel the responsibility to play a mentor role - to teach, educate and inform others about the practical use of existing and developing civil engineering computer technologies.

As a way to combine our interests in both software development and education, Haestad Methods began organizing workshops on the use and application of popular civil engineering design software packages including our own. We have since earned the highest attainable level of accreditation for continuing education through the IACET[1] and NSPE PDRES-certifications[2]. In 1997, Haestad Press debuted with the *1997 Practical Guide to Hydraulics and Hydrology* and both student and professional versions of our *Computer Applications in Hydraulic Engineering* textbook and academic CD-ROM. These books were followed in 1998 by the second edition of *Computer Applications* which contained several enhancements based on feedback from adopters of the original version.

Although the publications released by Haestad Press were gaining popularity, the promotion of Haestad Methods' products within the pages of the *Practical Guide* and in the marketing for both *Computer Applications* detracted from the urgency and importance of these texts. All three books, as promised, delivered vital information about the application of civil engineering theory to computer technology, but it was difficult to distinguish between Haestad Press, the publisher and Haestad Methods, the software developer.

I came to Haestad Methods from a civil engineering consulting firm. Like my new found colleagues who had started Haestad Press, I recognized that few civil engineers fully capitalize on the automation capabilities of existing computer technologies. This phenomenon – as my prior experience with engineering firms and municipalities around the United States lead me to conclude – was caused by the disturbing distance between the growth of civil engineering software and the availability of resources discussing the practical application of these tools to solve real-world engineering problems.

After reading and reviewing previous Haestad Press publications, I realized that in order to successfully embody the ideals on which it began, Haestad Press must exist as a separate entity from Haestad Methods. My time at Haestad has since been dedicated to developing Haestad Press as an independent company providing civil engineering professionals and students valuable resources necessary to bridge the gaps in their own understanding of how fundamental civil engineering theory can be applied to computer technology in practical, real-world situations.

Divided into four sections, *Essential Hydraulics and Hydrology* addresses topics from calibration with tracer studies and inlet design with the new FHWA standards to system optimization with genetic algorithms and the use of multimedia for product evaluation and continuing education. By combining discussions of both traditional theory and cutting-edge technology, *Essential Hydraulics and Hydrology* delivers the knowledge all civil engineers and engineering students must access in order to make sense of the diverse and rapid technological advances in their profession. In the next year, expect Haestad Press to be building momentum with further textbooks such as *Computer Assisted Water Distribution Modeling.*

Achieving the world-renowned quality of our computer applications and continuing education programs would be difficult without Haestad Methods' genuine interest in and dedication to the progress of civil engineering technology. Our engineers regularly engage and immerse themselves in discussion and debate about trends in civil engineering computer technology and education. Haestad Press was created as a logical extension of this passion for hydrology and hydraulics, providing a forum for our engineers and clients to share their ideas, theoretical and technical knowledge, and real-world experiences with the global civil engineering community. Anyone who loves their job and what they do as much as we do will certainly understand the need and desire for such an outlet.

In any discipline, progress can not be made without a forum for sharing ideas and debating vital issues and new approaches to solving age-old problems. Civil engineering periodicals, books, websites, Internet newsgroups and academic institutions all afford this opportunity but many often fail to address topics from a practical or technological standpoint. In the absence of such discussion, the gap between the rapid development of civil engineering design software and the civil engineers' ability to effectively utilize these tools increases at an dramatic rate. Haestad Press promises to bridge this gap by providing civil engineers with the knowledge and resources necessary to understand and master hydraulic and hydrologic engineering computer technology. *Essential Hydraulics and Hydrology* is only a taste of what's to come.

Adam Strafaci, Editor in Chief
November 1998

[1] International Association for Continuing Education and Training (www.iacet.org).
[2] Professional Development Registry for Engineers and Surveyors is a continuing education registry sponsored by the National Society of Professional Engineers (www.nspe.org/pdres).

Special Topics In Water Distribution Modeling

Use of Tracer Studies and Water Quality Models to Calibrate a Network Hydraulic Model

Overcome the limitations of traditional calibration methods with the use of tracer studies and water quality models.

M odel calibration is the process of adjusting model characteristics and parameters so that the model matches actual observed field data to some desirable level. Calibration would not be necessary if the mathematical model exactly represented the actual physical processes and we had perfect knowledge of all of the required parameters. We could then just apply the model with complete confidence that it would reproduce real world results. Unfortunately, neither of the criteria listed above are generally met, thus calibration is a necessary consideration in all studies.

This article will present the merits of an alternative calibration method which utilizes tracer studies and water quality models. The technique involves injecting a known substance (tracer) into the system and then calibrating by comparing water quality modeling results with manual concentration tests.

There are many excellent papers and discussions of calibration that have been published in the past few years. Herrin (1997a) provides an overview of the calibration process (reprinted in this book - see next article) and offers an example of this process (Herrin, 1997b). Walski (1995) discusses standards for model calibration and addresses the question of "when are we done with calibration?" Cesario, Kroon, Grayman, and Wright (1996) present perspectives on alternative calibration procedures around the world. Rossman (1997) addresses the issue of when a model has been sufficiently calibrated and tested to be put to predictive use. These papers provide valuable insights and suggestions on calibration.

Traditional Calibration Methods

Traditional methods for calibrating water distribution system models rely upon field measurements of system pressures, pipe flows, and water levels in storage facilities. The model is applied and various parameters are adjusted so that the model more closely represents the observed data. Parameters that are generally adjusted include: pipe roughness, pipe diameters (to account for the fact that actual pipe diameters differ from the nominal installed diameters), demands, and operational conditions such as valve position, pump curves, etc. Parameters should be kept within reasonable ranges and the set selected should result in the closest fit between predicted and observed data.

Limitations of Traditional Calibration Methods

A typical network representation of a water system includes hundreds or thousands of links and nodes. As indicated above, during the calibration process roughness coefficients and diameters may be adjusted for each link and demands may be adjusted for nodes. Typically, the number of field measurement sites (pressure, flow, or water levels) is limited to a relatively small number. In the UK, the traditional goal has been to test at least 30% of the nodes in the model. However, with the move away from skeletonization, the practicality of this goal has been questioned (Cesario et al, 1996). In the United States, the relative number of field measurements is significantly less than in the UK. As a result, there are generally a couple of orders of magnitude more parameters to be calibrated than there are field measurement sites. This disparity leads to a situation where there are many different sets of calibration parameters that could satisfy the same set of field conditions.

A second limitation of traditional calibration methods has arisen with the increasing popularity of water quality models used in association with the classical hydraulic models of distribution systems. In the more traditional uses of network models to assure adequate pressure in a distribution system, the goal is to develop a model which adequately predicts pressure. In water quality modeling, the model must also be a good predictor of flow and velocities since these characteristics ultimately effect the degree of decay and transformation of non-conservative constituents. The following discussion shows that a model that has been calibrated for pressures can still lead to incorrect velocities.

Friction head loss is usually predicted in network models using the Hazen-Williams head loss equation:

$$h_f = 3.02V^{1.85}L/C^{1.85}D^{1.165}$$
(U.S. Customary units)

$$h_f = 6.79V^{1.85}L/C^{1.85}D^{1.165}$$
(Metric units)

Where:

h_f = headloss due to friction (ft, m)
V = velocity (ft/s, m/s)
L = pipe length (ft, m)
C = Hazen-Williams friction coefficient
D = pipe diameter (ft, m)

As Figure 1-1 illustrates, there are many combinations of the Hazen-Williams C-value and the pipe diameter that will lead to the same predicted head loss in the pipe. For example, a C-value of 83 and a pipe diameter of 12" results in

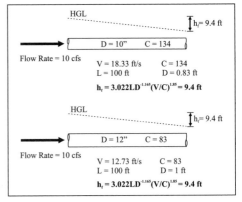

Figure 1-1: Example of C-value/diameter combinations

the same head loss as a C-value of 134 and a pipe diameter of 10". In a traditional process where pressures are being matched, the normal procedure is to assume the nominal pipe diameter and to select the C-value that results in the best match for pressure. This approach leads to an acceptable calibration for pressure prediction. However, if the nominal diameters are incorrect due to pipe fabrication, encrustation, or corrosion, then pressures may be accurately predicted but will result in errors in velocity predictions. As a result, the calibration that is adequate for pressure prediction may not be adequate for velocity prediction.

Tracer Studies and Water Quality Modeling as a Calibration Method

An alternative or supplementary method for calibrating network models utilizes tracer studies of the distribution system in conjunction with network hydraulic and water quality models. All water quality models of distribution systems depend upon hydraulic models to provide information on pipe flows, flow directions, and flow velocities. Inaccuracies in the flow/velocity values provided by the hydraulic model will lead to inaccuracies in water quality predictions.

Although most water quality models can be used to represent both conservative and non-conservative substances, the use of conservative substances are most appropriate for the calibration of hydraulic models. When modeling a conservative substance, there are

An alternative or supplementary method for calibrating network models utilizes tracer studies of the distribution system in conjunction with network hydraulic and water quality models.

essentially no water quality parameters that need to be adjusted. In other words, if the hydraulic parameters are correct and the initial conditions and loading conditions for the substance are accurately known, then the water quality model should provide a good estimate of the concentration of the substance throughout the network. The use of the water quality model and conservative tracer as a means of calibrating the hydraulic model is based upon this relationship.

Steps in Applying the Tracer Calibration Method

The calibration process using water quality modeling may be summarized as follows:

1) A conservative tracer is identified for a distribution system. The tracer may be a chemical that is added to the flow at an appropriate location or, for the situation where there are multiple sources of water, may be a naturally occurring difference in the water sources such as hardness. Chemicals that are typically used include fluoride, calcium chloride, sodium chloride and lithium chloride. Selection of the tracer generally depends upon government regulations (e.g., some localities will not allow the use of fluoride), the availability and cost of the chemicals, the methods for adding the chemical to the system, and the measuring/analysis devices.

2) A controlled field experiment is performed where one of the following occurs: the conservative tracer is injected into the system for a prescribed period of time; a conservative substance that is normally added such as

fluoride is shut off for a prescribed period of time; a naturally occurring substance that differs between sources is traced.

3) During the planning stage for a tracer study, the distribution system model should be applied to the study area under the conditions that are expected during the tracer study. The model can be used to predict the likely movement of the tracer through the system and assist in selecting both sampling sites and frequency. Although the model is not fully calibrated at this stage, the information gained from running the model is valuable in planning the tracer study.

4) During the field experiment, the concentration of the tracer is measured at selected locations in the distribution system along with other parameters that are required by a hydraulic model such as tank water levels, pump operations, flows, etc. Sampling locations should be selected based on both their representativeness and their accessibility. They should be spread around the study area and reflect locations where the data will be of interest. Care must be taken to adequately flush the sampling taps to insure that water is being drawn from the main. Though permanent sampling taps are the easiest to use, hydrants and locations that are available around the clock may also be sampled. In addition to the conservative tracer, other water quality concentrations may be measured such as chlorine residual, though these values are not generally used in the calibration process.

The model can be used to predict the likely movement of the tracer through the system and assist in selecting both sampling sites and frequency.

5) The model is then run with alternative hydraulic parameter values to determine the model parameters that result in the best representation of the field data. Perhaps, traditional pressure and flow measurements are used to perform a first-step calibration. The water quality model is then used to model the conservative tracer.

6) Good agreement between the predicted and observed tracer concentrations indicates a good calibration of the hydraulic model for the conditions being modeled. Significant deviations between the observed and modeled concentrations indicate that further calibration of the hydraulic model is required. Various statistical and directed search techniques may be used in conjunction with the conservative tracer data to aid the user in adjusting the hydraulic model parameters so as to better match the observed concentrations.

Example Applications

Brushy Plains, Connecticut

A frequently cited tracer and calibration study was performed in 1991 in the Brushy Plains Service Area of the South Central Connecticut Regional Water Authority (SCCRWA) system in the New Haven, Connecticut region (Rossman, Clark and Grayman, 1994). This service area is composed of a 2 square mile residential area in the eastern part of the SCCRWA system. Water is pumped into the service area by the Cherry Hill Pump Station located at the southern end of the service area. Storage in the service area is provided by a 1 million gallon, 70 foot high tank. During normal operation, the pumps are set to go on when the water height in the tank drops to 56 feet and to turn off when the water height reaches 65 feet.

A skeletonized representation of the system (Figure 1-2) was developed which included all 12-inch mains, major 8-inch mains and loops, and pipes that connected to the sampling sites. A Hazen-Williams roughness coefficient of 100 was assumed for all pipes. Nodal demand patterns were estimated based on the number of structures of different types in conjunction with an average water use by structures.

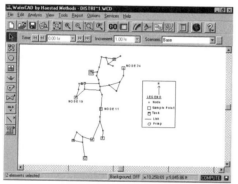

Figure 1-2: Schematic of Brushy Plains water distribution system

Fluoride was selected as the tracer for the study. Since fluoride is routinely added to the SCCRWA water, the fluoride feed at the treatment plant was shut off for a period of 47-hours and sampling was performed in the distribution system. Samples were taken at seven distribution sampling sites in addition to samples at the pump station (on the effluent side) and along the line leading to the tank. Samples were analyzed for both fluoride (for calibration) and chlorine.

The network hydraulic-water quality model was subsequently run for the conditions observed during the sampling study. Initial results indicated significant discrepancies between predicted and observed fluoride concentrations. Model parameters that were then adjusted included pipe roughness coefficients and spatial and temporal demand patterns. Following the calibration process, excellent agreement was found for sampling stations located on the main transmission lines in the service area (e.g., node 11). Improvements were found in the smaller and dead-end lines (e.g., nodes 19 and 34) though discrepancies still remained after the calibration process. The observed and predicted fluoride concentrations following calibration for three representative nodes are shown in Figure 1-3.

Other Examples

The tracer/water quality modeling technique has been employed in several studies around the world to assist in calibrating hydraulic models. Grayman, Clark, and Males (1988) describe a study in the North Penn Water Authority distribution system in which sampling data of the naturally occurring differences in hardness and trihalomethane (THM) concentrations in the various ground water and surface water sources were used in the validation of a hydraulic model. THM's had reached their full formation potential so that they could be treated as a conservative substance. Clark et al (1991) describe a study in which fluoride was shut off for a 7-day period in the Cheshire region of the South Central Connecticut Regional Water Authority system with field data collected over the subsequent 2-week period. Both the transient period after fluoride was shut off and the transient period when fluoride injection was restarted were used in the calibration process.

In a study sponsored by the AWWA Research Foundation, Vasconcelos et al (1996) used several different tracers to calibrate or validate hydraulic models as part of a study of chlorine decay dynamics in distribution systems. Fluoride was injected as a tracer in a study of the Oberlin portion

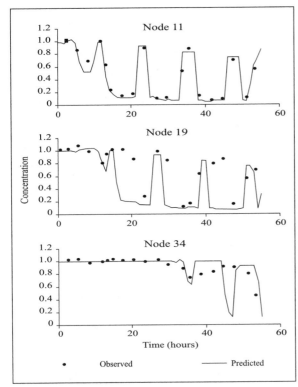

Figure 1-3: Observed and predicted fluoride concentrations

provided an excellent conservative tracer to use in the calibration of the hydraulic model.

Conclusions

Tracer studies and water quality models have been used in many applications as part of the calibration process of hydraulic models of small and medium sized distribution systems. To date, the tracer studies have involved manual collection and analysis of the samples. In order to increase the practicality of the method and to extend it to larger systems, development of inexpensive, automated monitors is required. The technology exists for such monitors but increased user demand is needed to encourage packaging of a low-cost field unit.

Author: Walter M. Grayman, Ph.D., PE

of the Dauphin system near Harrisburg, PA. The Oberlin section is an isolated 1-square mile service area. Dauphin does not normally fluoridate and in order to minimize pipe wall demand, fluoride was added for a 7-day period prior to the study. The fluoride feed was then discontinued and hourly fluoride measurements were made at 30 sites in the study area. The resulting detailed data set was used to refine the calibration of the hydraulic model of the area.

The North Marin, California distribution system receives water from two surface water sources. Sodium hydroxide is normally added at one source resulting in a sodium concentration of around 23 mg/l while the naturally occurring sodium level in the other source is around 9 mg/l. This

The Fundamentals of Calibration

Gain confidence in your model by bringing it into agreement with recorded field conditions. Calibration is your best guarantee that the model represents the real system.

A pipe distribution network model is created from a combination of assumptions, modeling judgment and best guesses based on theoretical information. Obviously, this will not always generate results that agree perfectly with a non-theoretical, real-world system.

Calibration is the process of adjusting the characteristics of the water distribution model to better reflect the behavior of the real system. The process of calibration may include changing system demands, fine-tuning pipe roughnesses, altering pump operating characteristics, or any number of other things that affect the performance of the model.

The Significance of Calibration

The calibration process is a necessary and important operation for several reasons:

- **Confidence**. Calibration demonstrates the model's ability to reproduce existing conditions

(thereby increasing the confidence in the model to predict future conditions).

- **Understanding**. Calibration also acts as an excellent introduction to the performance of the system, familiarizing the modeler with the changing behavior of the network caused by alterations to different components.

- **Troubleshooting**. One area of calibration that is often overlooked is the ability to uncover missing information or misinformation about the system (such as incorrect pipe diameters or closed valves).

Collecting Field Data

Collecting field data is a large part of the calibration process, because without field data there is nothing to compare the model to. Data collection is usually separated into three categories:

- Physical Data

- Operational Data

- Reactive Data

Physical Data

This category includes verification of many system characteristics that are already known (or are thought to be known) and that are used to create the base model. Examples of these data are:

- Pipe roughness
- Pump head and discharge characteristics
- Regulating valve behavior
- Tank diameters, elevations, etc.
- Control switch settings

These are the data that set the physical guidelines for how the system will react to a variety of conditions. If these data are not represented accurately in the model, it will be impossible to achieve a high level of confidence.

Operational Data

Operational data are collected by continuously monitoring the system, usually for a week or two. Important areas to observe include:

- Flow and water surface elevation readings at the boundary locations (groundwater wells, treatment facilities, storage tanks, etc.)
- Flow and pressure readings at other key locations within the system (regulating valves, pump stations, etc.)
- Demands for high-consumption customers

The best locations to collect operational data can often be determined by observing the base model, even in a noncalibrated condition. The model can be used to predict which components of the system are the most sensitive to changes in the input data and are therefore the most crucial components to monitor.

Operational data, like physical data, are often collected during the development of the base model.

Reactive Data

Reactive data are gathered by stressing the system to simulate a fire flow, power outage or other extreme situation (provided this will not damage the system or adversely affect the system's customers). If a good base model has been developed from the physical and operational data, it can be used to predict the best field locations for performing reactive testing.

At the time of testing, boundary conditions, flowrates and pressures are recorded at various key locations throughout the system. These values may be recorded instantaneously for use in a steady-state calibration or they can be tracked over time for an extended-period calibration.

One of the most common places to monitor the system and control the testing process is through a fire hydrant (Figure 1-4). A hydrant is readily accessible, and flows and pressures can be measured with appropriate equipment. Fire flow testing requires at least two points of access to the distribution system:

- **Flow Hydrant.** This is the hydrant that is actually opened, discharging enough water to create measurable pressure drops in the system. If one open hydrant does not create a large enough drop, additional hydrants in the area can be opened to generate larger flows. Flow is typically measured using a pitot gauge – an instrument that is placed in the discharge stream.

- **Pressure Hydrant.** This hydrant is used to record static and residual pressures, since pressures at the flow hydrant fluctuate too much to obtain reliable readings. The pressure hydrant should be in the same vicinity as the flow hydrant to ensure that the pressure drop is a direct result of the opened hydrant.

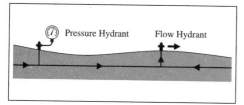

Figure 1-4: Hydrant flow test

The incentive behind reactive testing is to observe the system under stressed conditions, so a test time should be picked that is close to the maximum demand that the system usually sees. For most systems, this kind of testing would be performed between 2 p.m. and 6 p.m. during the hottest week of the summer.

Adjusting the Model

The most time consuming part of calibrating a model is the process of making adjustments to the model, in order to bring it into agreement with the field results. If the base model has the correct physical data, the adjustment process consists primarily of making iterative changes to pipe roughnesses and junction demands.

The guidelines for making adjustments are fairly simple and relate directly to the characteristics of a pipe. When the flow is greater, or when there is more roughness, the pipe will have more headloss. Based on this relationship, actions can be taken to adjust the model.

If the model hydraulic grade lines (HGL) are *higher* than field recorded values (Figure 1-5): This indicates that the model is not predicting enough headloss. To produce larger headlosses, roughen the pipes or increase junction demands.

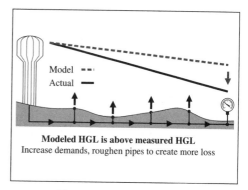

Modeled HGL is above measured HGL
Increase demands, roughen pipes to create more loss

Figure 1-5: Modeled HGL too high

If the model hydraulic grades are *lower* than field recorded values (Figure 1-6): This indicates that the model is predicting too much headloss. To produce smaller headlosses, smooth the pipes or decrease junction demands.

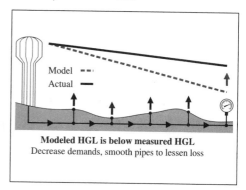

Modeled HGL is below measured HGL
Decrease demands, smooth pipes to lessen loss

Figure 1-6: Modeled HGL too low

Working with Data Comparisons

When comparisons are done between field results and modeled results, there is no mathematical reason to use pressures instead of hydraulic grades, or vice versa. Because pressure is just a converted representation of the height of the hydraulic grade line above the ground elevation, the two are essentially equivalent for comparison purposes.

For model management, however, there are several compelling arguments for working with hydraulic grades rather than pressures:

- Hydraulic grades provide the modeler with a sense of the accuracy and reliability of the data. If one hydraulic grade value is drastically different from another, it should immediately signal to the modeler that there might be erroneous data. Unless the ground is perfectly flat, pressure differences are not as easily noticed (because elevation changes alone can cause significant pressure changes).

- Hydraulic grades give an indication of the direction of flow (from higher grade to lower). This information can give the modeler further insight into the behavior of the network – insight that pressures do not provide.

- Working with hydraulic grades relaxes the modeler's need for precise elevations at the test locations. The elevation at which the test measurements are taken might not be the same as the elevation that is chosen for the modeled junction node. Dealing with pressures could result in a discrepancy, but hydraulic grade comparisons avoid this problem.

In essence, hydraulic grade or pressure comparisons will both lead to the same results if all other factors are equal. Pressure comparisons make it much easier to overlook errors, however, and also make it much harder to track down inconsistencies between the field and the model. Working with hydraulic grades does not require any additional effort, but it can have large time-savings during calibration troubleshooting.

Troubleshooting

In an ideal world, measured field data and predicted model results would match perfectly every time. Unfortunately, the real world is far from perfect, and models can produce results that do not match field values. In fact, the model results may be so far away from the field measurements that simple errors in roughness and demand estimation can not possibly account for the differences.

Differences between the field results and model results can obviously only come from two places: blunders in the input data (such as typographical errors or other mistakes in transcribing the data into the model); or incorrect field data (incorrect pipe diameters, closed valves or other inaccurate assumptions). Double-checking the input data for the model against the source of information is a straightforward way of ruling out typographical blunders, but tracking down incorrect field data can be much more difficult.

Using the Model to Locate Errors in the Field

Before rushing out in the field randomly searching for closed valves or other problems, try using the model to focus on where the uncertainty is originating. Try opening or closing a pipe, turning a pump on or off or adjusting a valve. This process only takes a few minutes and can save both time and money in the field by narrowing the scope of the troubleshooting effort.

Allowable Error?

Do not confuse the term "error" with the term "blunder." Blunders (human mistakes) are only one type of error and are not the *only* source of disagreement between field measurements and model results. Other errors can come from pressure gauge readings, estimated water demands, and random variations in the system conditions.

Every model will have some level of error because of the imprecision in assumed conditions and available modeling techniques. It is unreasonable to expect a model to agree exactly with field data for every condition. The objective of creating a model is to generate a tool for predicting network behavior to a tolerable accuracy level, not to perfection.

Minimizing Errors
by Calibrating Extremes

Errors within the model will be exaggerated at higher flowrates. Differences at very low flowrates usually indicate errors in junction elevation or reservoir water surface levels. At higher flowrates, (Figure 1-7) larger errors occur because pipe headloss is related exponentially to the flowrate (usually by a power of about 2).

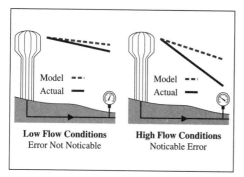

Low Flow Conditions
Error Not Noticable

High Flow Conditions
Noticable Error

Figure 1-7: Exaggerated error at high flowrate

These exaggerated headlosses demonstrate the importance of focusing on times when the network is under high demand stress, because these measurements provide larger headlosses for comparison against the model. A model that is calibrated for peak demand conditions can be used

in confidence to model low demand conditions – a model that is calibrated for low demand conditions can not be extended with as much confidence to model peak demand conditions.

Reprinted from Haestad Press's 1997 Practical Guide to Hydraulics and Hydrology.

Author: Gregg A. Herrin

Key Concepts

- Calibration is the process of adjusting the model until it agrees with the behavior of the real system.

- A model of an existing system should always be calibrated before it is used for any serious design or analysis purposes. An uncalibrated model may be able to give the modeler a "ballpark" feel for the behavior of the system, but the results should absolutely *not* be misinterpreted as being fully representative of the actual system.

- It is important to gather information regarding the system's physical data (pipe roughness, tank elevations, etc.), operational data (pressure switch settings, flow readings, etc.) and reactive data (fire flow tests).

- Many of the model characteristics can be adjusted during calibration, including pipe roughness and junction demands.

- The model can actually be used in some instances to track down problems, such as a closed pipe or throttled valve that the modeler did not originally know about.

- Calibrating to extreme conditions helps minimize errors in the model.

Importance and Accuracy of Node Elevation Data

Make educated decisions on your data collection method by understanding how node elevation data is used in a water distribution model.

Obtaining node elevation data for input into a water distribution model can be an expensive, time-consuming process. While in some cases it may be well worth the effort and it is critical for the usefulness of the model, in other cases it can represent a significant effort with very little payback. In order to decide on the appropriate level of quality of elevation data to be gathered, it is important to understand how a model uses this data.

Elevation data for nodes are not directly used in solving the network equations in hydraulic models. Instead, the models actually solve for hydraulic grade line (HGL). Once the HGL is calculated and the numerical solution process is essentially completed, then the elevations are used to determine pressure using the following relationship.

$$P = (HGL - z)\rho\, g$$

Where:

P = pressure $(lb/ft^2, N/m^2)$
HGL = hydraulic grade line (ft, m)

z = node elevation (ft, m)
ρ = density of water $(slugs/ft^3, kg/m^3)$
g = gravitational acceleration $(ft/s^2, m/s^2)$

If the modeler is only interested in calculating flows, velocities, and HGL values, then he or she need not specify elevation. In this case the pressures at the nodes will be computed assuming an elevation of zero, thus resulting in pressures relative to a zero elevation.

Of course, if the modeler specifies pump controls or pressure valve settings in pressure units, then the model needs to compute pressures relative to the elevation of the nodes being tested. In this case, the elevation at the control node or control valve would need to be specified (or else the model will assume zero elevation). In short, an accurate elevation value is required at each key node where pressure is of importance.

Numerical Value of Elevation

What is meant by the correct elevation of a node? Is it the centerline elevation of the pipe in the ground? Is it the ground surface elevation? Is it the elevation of the hydrant outlet where pressure is measured? Is it the elevation of the customer's meter or faucet? The correct answer is that the node elevation is the elevation at which the modeler wants to know the pressure.

The relationship between pressure and elevation is illustrated in Figure 1-8. Notice that the HGL of 400 ft. calculated at the location of this hydrant is independent of elevation. However, depending on which elevation the modeler entered for that node, the pressure can vary as shown. Usually model users use ground elevation as the elevation for the node, but an argument can be made for using any of the other possible alternatives.

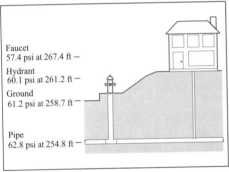

Figure 1-8: Relationship between pressure and elevation at a constant HGL of 400 feet

Accuracy and Precision

The next question usually posed regarding elevation data is the requirement for accuracy. That is, how accurate must the elevation data be? The answer boils down to a tradeoff between the accuracy desired in pressure calculations vs. the amount of labor (and cost) allotted for data collection.

For the sake of this discussion, assume that the HGL calculated by the model is significantly more precise than any elevation data. Because 2.31 ft of elevation corresponds to 1 psi of pressure (for water), calculating pressure to 1 psi precision requires elevation data accurate to roughly 2 ft. Elevation data that is accurate to the nearest 10 ft will result in pressure that is accurate to roughly 4 psi.

The modeler needs to keep the precision of pressure results in mind when presenting the results of modeling studies. If the pressure is only known to plus or minus 4 psi, then the tables of results should not contain values such as 61.421psi. The last three digits in such a number are meaningless and somewhat misleading. Some models, such as Cybernet® and WaterCAD®, allow precision to be controlled for report purposes.

The lack of precision in elevation data (and hence pressure results), also leads to some interesting questions regarding water distribution design. If design criteria states that pressure must exceed 20 psi and the model gives a pressure of 21 +/- 4 psi or 19 +/- 4 psi, the engineer relying on the model will have to decide if their design is acceptable.

Obtaining Elevation Data

In building the large models used today, collecting elevation data is often a time consuming process. A good modeler wants to devote the appropriate level of effort to data collection that will yield the desired accuracy at a minimum cost. Some of the data collection options are:

- USGS Topographic Maps

- Surveying from Known Benchmarks

- Digital Elevation Models (DEMs)

- Digital Ortho-Rectified Photogrammetry

- Contour Maps

- As-Built Plans

- Global Positioning Systems

USGS Topographic Maps

United States Geological Survey (USGS) topographic maps are the most commonly used source for elevation data. In most locations they are produced at a 1:24000 scale and have contour lines at 20 ft intervals. Depending on the continuity of the slope between contour lines, interpolating elevations between contour lines yields elevations that are accurate to roughly 10 ft. If the slopes are continuous, then better accuracy is possible. Conversely, if there are abrupt changes in slope, the accuracy can be less. If the modeler is familiar with the area, interpolation errors can be reduced.

Such accuracy may be acceptable for most nodes in a model as long as the user appreciates the limitations in pressure calculations. Better elevation data should be obtained for key nodes such as pressure reducing valves and pumps.

Surveying From Known Benchmarks

The most accurate way to obtain elevation data is to survey the desired points starting at known benchmarks. However, this is a very costly and time consuming approach and is usually only justified for some critical points such as the centerline of a pump or the pressure transducer elevation at a monitoring point. In most cases, the elevation of such points should already be known from as-built plans.

Digital Elevation Models

Digital Elevation Models (DEMs), available from the USGS, are computer files that contain elevation data and routines for interpolating that data to arrive at elevations at nearby points. DEM data are recorded in a raster mode which means that they are represented by uniform grid cells of a specified resolution (typically 30 m). The accuracy of points interpolated from the grid depends on the distance from known benchmarks and is highly site specific. However, it is usually on the order of 5 to 10 ft when the ground slopes continuously. If there are abrupt breaks in elevation corresponding to road cuts, levees, and cliffs, the elevations taken from the DEMs can be significantly inaccurate.

Digital Ortho Photogrammetry

Elevations can be determined from stereo aerial photographs. These photos need to be corrected for parallax effects, curvature of the earth, and atmospheric interferences and tied to known benchmarks. Once this data has been orthorectified, it can be viewed on a computer monitor using special glasses to produce a 3-D image. Pointing and clicking on any point will give the elevation of that point to an accuracy on the order of one foot or better depending on the elevation from which the photos were taken and the quality of the ground control. Obtaining and processing the photographs is expensive (on the order of $5000 to $10,000 per square mile) so it is difficult to justify the cost for modeling purposes alone. However, it may be possible to pool resources from others interested in such data to reduce the costs to each party.

Contour Maps

The USGS topographic maps are not the only kind of contour map that can be produced. The information from digital photogrammetry

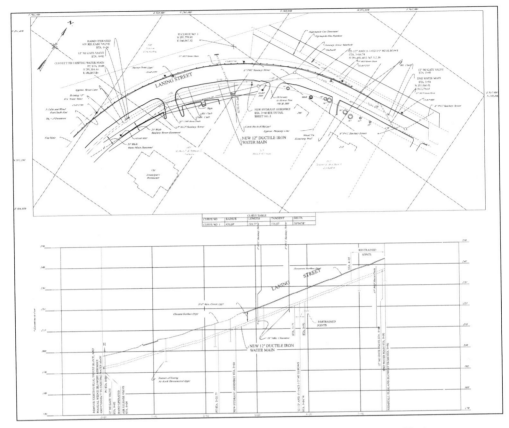

Figure 1-9: Sample as-built drawing of pipe layout (compliments of Roald Haestad Inc.)

described above can be used to generate contour maps to accuracies of better than one foot. For modeling purposes, maps with a contour interval of two feet are sufficient. This usually results in pressure accuracies better than 1 psi without being too cluttered. In ordering these maps, the scale must be such that the contours are not too close together while also making sure that an excessive number of sheets are not required.

As-Built Plans

As-built (i.e. record) plans of pipe layout such as the one shown in Figure 1-9 can also serve as an accurate source of elevation data. The downside is

that elevations are not always shown on water distribution record drawings and the drawings are not always easily accessible. Furthermore, as-built plans are not always up-to-date and therefore, may not accurately represent field conditions.

While elevation data are not critical in laying water mains, elevations are very important for sewer mains. Most sewage collection utilities have maps with accurate elevations of manhole covers or can readily locate plan and profile drawings for most of their mains. Street and highway departments and agencies that review subdivisions should also have good elevation data in their records. The problem with using as-builts as the source of elevation data

---

is that it usually takes a great deal of time to find the right drawing. However, as more agencies and utilities are digitizing drawings and linking these images to Geographic Information Systems (GIS), as-built drawings may prove to be a better source of data in the future.

Global Positioning Systems

Global Positioning Systems (GPS) are the most promising new technology for determining elevations. A GPS uses signals from satellites to determine the location of a point in three dimensions. In order to use a GPS, it is necessary to physically occupy the location with a GPS receiver unit.

Not all GPS receiver units are equivalent in accuracy. Code phase processing can only be expected to produce a vertical accuracy on the order of 10 ft. Carrier phase processing can give an accuracy on the order of 1 ft provided the receiver is reasonably close to the base station. Mountains, tall structures, and the positioning of satellites can also cause problems with a GPS. Furthermore, the accuracy also depends on the length of time a point is occupied. It may be necessary to occupy a point for up to 15 minutes without interruption to achieve the optimal accuracy. Higher levels of accuracy are attained with the use of multiple satellites (Figure 1-10). GPS technology is improving each year and shows great promise as a source for elevation data.

Datum

When collecting elevation data, it is important to know which datum is being used. The two most common datum used in the United States are the National Geodetic Vertical Datum of 1929 and the North American Vertical Datum of 1988. However, it is not uncommon to find several datum differing by as much as 10 ft in a given area. This is especially problematic when using as-built drawings as the source for elevation data because design engineers are more interested in the relative accuracy of elevations within their project as opposed to absolute elevations.

Age of Data

It is also helpful to know the date corresponding to elevation data taken from maps. In certain areas, there can be significant subsidence due to mining activity and groundwater extraction. Elevations may also change due to grading during land development or reclamation projects.

Calibration Nodes

An elevation accuracy of 5 ft is adequate for most nodes; therefore, a USGS topographic map is typically acceptable. However, for nodes to be used for model calibration, a higher level of accuracy is desirable.

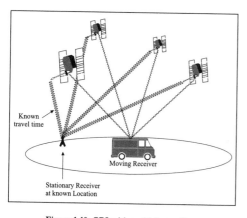

Figure 1-10: GPS with multiple satellites

Consider a situation where both the model and the actual system have exactly the same HGL of 800 ft at a node (Figure 1-11). The elevation of the

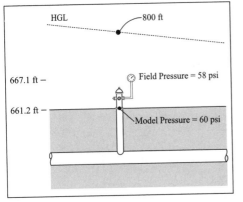

Figure 1-11: Importance of elevation at calibration nodes

ground (and model node) is 661.2 ft while the elevation of the pressure gage used in calibration is at elevation 667.1 ft. The model would predict a pressure of 60.1 psi while the gage would read 57.5 psi even though the model is exactly correct at this point.

A similar error could occur in the opposite direction with an incorrect pressure appearing accurate because an incorrect elevation is used. This is one reason why model calibration should be done by comparing modeled and observed HGL values and not pressures. In any case, the elevations used for calibration data collection should be held to a higher standard of accuracy than other nodes in the model.

Summary

Collecting elevation data is one of the more straightforward but tedious tasks in model building. By understanding how the data are used and what the data sources are, the modeler will hopefully select the best and most cost effective approach for gathering elevation data.

Author: Thomas Walski, Ph.D., PE

Special thanks to Bill Toothill of the Wilkes University GIS/ Remote Sensing Center for providing information on GPS and mapping.

Relating Design Flow, Pipe Size, and Cost

*Find the balance between sound planning
and financial responsibility.*

No one would deny that the determination of design flow is extremely important in the selection of a pipe size and the cost of a water distribution project. It would seem that all one has to do is select a design flow for a pipe to calculate the optimal size (i.e. lowest cost) rather easily. Unfortunately, the problem is not quite that simple. This article will look at the relationship between design flow and cost, and describe the implications of assumptions about design flow on pipe size.

Numerous papers (something on the order of 200) have been published over the years on techniques to optimally size pipes. Most of these techniques can provide some insight into pipe sizing and some even show promise in becoming practical engineering tools. However, practicing engineers have typically not embraced these tools and are still relying, to a great extent, on engineering judgment for pipe sizing decisions. The following is a list of reasons why optimal sizing of pipes has not been widely accepted.

practicing engineers...are still relying, to a great extent, on engineering judgement for pipe sizing decisions .

- Optimization models are generally not user friendly.

- Engineers are more interested in a reliable system and are willing to sacrifice savings for greater reliability and some capacity for growth.

- Demand usually does not reach the design value instantly, but gradually over many years.

- There is really no such thing as a single "design flow" for a given pipe.

- There is a great deal of uncertainty in estimating future demands.

It is only a matter of time before the usability of optimization models is improved. However, addressing the other four reasons for the nonacceptance of pipe size optimization is much more problematic.

Basic Relationships

First lets examine the relationship between design flow, pipe size, and cost. The relationship between the flow a pipe carries and its diameter is given in numerous equations including the Hazen-Williams equation.

$$Q = 0.432CD^{2.63}S^{0.54}$$
(U.S. customary units)

$$Q = 0.278CD^{2.63}S^{0.54}$$
(SI units)

Where:

Q = flowrate (ft³/s, m³/s)

C = Hazen-Williams Coefficient

D = pipe diameter (ft, m)

S = slope of energy grade line (ft/ft, m/m)

The cost of piping is very site specific, but all other things being equal, the cost of installed water mains varies from roughly the 1.4 to 1.6 power of the pipe diameter (Walski, 1984).

$$\text{Pipe Cost} \approx (\text{Pipe Diameter})^{1.4 \to 1.6}$$

Combining these two relationships results in the following approximation for pipe cost.

$$\text{Pipe Cost} \approx Q^{0.5}$$

Of course there are many things that affect this relationship, the most significant of which is the fact that pipes are only available in discrete diameter (did you ever try to buy a 17.2 in. pipe?).

The cost of installed water mains varies from roughly the 1.4 to 1.6 power of the pipe diameter.

Therefore, in some cases, increasing the design flow may not have an affect on cost while in others, a tiny change in design flow can make a huge difference in cost. However, for larger variations in design flow, the relationship between cost and design flow can be summarized by the following rule of thumb:

$$\% \ \Delta \ \text{cost} = 0.5 \ (\% \ \Delta \ \text{design flow})$$

This means that a 10% change in design flow will yield approximately a 5% change in cost while a 50% change in design flow will yield approximately a 25% change in cost. This all sounds pretty easy. The real problem is determining the actual design flow.

Design Flow

The design flow in a pipe is pretty easy to figure out, right? The engineer simply looks into the future and determines the greatest flow that the pipe will need to carry. What is so hard about that? The hard part is looking into the future. Obviously, most engineers (and people in general) are not very good at this. The key of course is to hire a psychic with a degree in hydraulics and let this individual come up with the design flow.

Engineers are a rational and skeptical bunch so they are not very likely to rely on psychics for their design calculations. It is, therefore, up to the engineers with the planners and managers from the utility company to come up with design flows and pipe sizes.

Engineers usually look at the initial use of the pipe and conclude that the design flow will be something like the flow that is needed when the pipe is installed, only greater by some amount. If the pipe serves a residential subdivision, that subdivision will have the same demand in the distant future. If it provides flow to a new factory, that factory will keep running at the same production for the life of the pipe. If it provides fire protection for a new school, that demand won't change. In a 5 to 10 year time frame, this sort of logic works pretty well and it is usually a long enough time for the engineer to move on to a new position.

However, let's stand back and take a look at design flows over a longer time frame. Returning 50 years later, the neighborhood has been replaced by high rise apartments, the manufacturing operation has been moved overseas, and the school has expanded three times. The actual demand in the vicinity of these pipes is nowhere near what was expected.

Did the engineer mess up? No, the engineer did the best that could be expected. The problem is that there is really no such thing as a single design flow in the life of a pipe and even if there was, the design engineer would not be able to know it beforehand. The sources of uncertainty are many, but are mostly tied to the vagaries of the economy, weather, developer investments, new technology, human behavior, and catastrophes.

The design flow is actually a stochastic kind of concept which makes it difficult to pinpoint precisely. A good way to visualize this is to look at a cumulative probability plot as shown in Figure 1-12. A point on this graph (e.g. 2000 gpm, 50%) means that there is a 50% chance that the flow of 2000 gpm will be exceeded during the life of the pipe. Those who think there is a concept such as a single correct design flow visualize this plot as the nearly vertical line. In reality, the design flow is really like the sloping line meaning there is a great deal of uncertainty in design flow before a pipe size is selected.

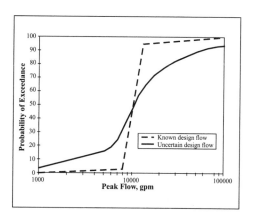

Figure 1-12: Cumulative probability plot

Self-Fulfilling Prophecy

This leads to another odd feature of design flow in that it is a form of a "self-fulfilling prophecy." Following the saying, "if you build it, they will come," once a utility company installs a pipe, it is reasonable to expect that its capacity will eventually be used•up. If the utility installs a pipe with 1500 gpm of capacity, some day that pipe will carry that flow and very little extra. Thus, before a pipe is sized there is no such thing as a "design flow" because pipe size determines design flow.

One of the weaknesses of the automated optimization of pipe sizing is that it tends to weed out capacity for future growth even though this capacity will be valuable in the future at very little cost today. It is amusing to look at papers about optimization of water distribution design and see places where the optimization routine has necked down a pipe at mid-block to save a few pennies even though a little extra expenditure could provide a great deal of additional capacity.

Uncertainty and Capacity

Real utilities do not work in a world of certainty. Whenever a pipe sizing decision is made, there is almost always a debate as to the basis for sizing the pipe. Does the utility simply size the pipe for the next customer or does it anticipate demands 5, 10, 20 or 50 years down the road? Most optimization schemes are not set up to recognize or handle this uncertainty in a practical way.

Rather than using the logic of optimization and asking the question, "what is the cheapest pipe we can install to meet known demands," experienced utility engineers look at the long term and ask questions with financial implications such as, "how much pipe can we justifiably install here and still get a good return on our investment and be fair to current rate payers." Optimization views capacity for growth as an evil which must be eliminated while practicing engineers see this capacity, in reasonable amounts, as an asset.

The rule of thumb stated earlier relating cost and capacity says that spending an extra 10% on a project can bring 20% extra capacity. The controlling factor in design, therefore, is not to eliminate capacity for growth. Rather, it is that there is only a limited amount of investment that current revenues can support, and the utility can not speculate too much on growth.

Staging and Growth

There is no standard value for the design life of a pipe. Some fail in ten years while others are providing satisfactory service after 120 years. Examining a single design flow can not account for the changes that occur over such a long period of time. Selecting a pipe that appears optimal in one time window may yield a pipe that is too expensive to lay today and will fail shortly after the window.

Significant judgment is needed to balance financial responsibility and the desire to make the best decision.

Fortunately, an incorrect decision is not usually fatal. If a pipe is "too large" by whatever standard used, that capacity will someday be used. If it is too small, it will always be possible to parallel or loop the pipe at a later date to provide the needed capacity.

Modeling Implications

If the engineer does not really know the design flow, it may seem to some that it is not worthwhile performing much analysis on the pipe sizing decision. On the contrary, in a world of uncertainty, the modeler must not only look at a single design flow but a wide range of design flows — the kind of multiple analyses that make easy-to-use models especially valuable. Instead of narrowing the analysis in on a single design flow, the engineer needs to be asking "what if the actual flows are 50% greater or less, and if so, what are the implications on system cost?" It is in making these repeated runs for a range of scenarios that an easy-to-use model can pay for itself.

Author: Thomas Walski, Ph.D., PE

Interpreting
Extended Period
Simulation Models

Make the most of your extended period
simulation modeling results.

Steady state water distribution models are the most commonly used tool in the engineer's arsenal for water supply system design. They can answer a wide variety of questions on pipe and pump sizing and system layout. However, there are some studies where steady state models are of limited use and extended period simulation (EPS) models are required. Some examples of these problems include:

- checking tank volumes,

- evaluating pump cycling for tank filling and draining,

- analyzing energy usage,

- preparing for special operations such as emergencies or shutdowns, and

- serving as a starting point for water quality models.

In using steady state modeling, the engineer tends to focus on the worst case situation (maximum day or catastrophic fire) since these usually control design. However, water system operation is not truly steady and in looking only at worst case situations, the engineer may miss some other problems (e.g. tank refilling or over pressurizing some areas). EPS runs provide a way to identify such problems.

This article will discuss how to use EPS models with an emphasis on what to look for in reviewing EPS output.

EPS Setup

Duration

Among the most basic questions in setting up EPS runs are how long should the run be and how many time steps should the run be divided into.

The duration of the run needs to be long enough to capture the events of interest. Many modelers use 24-hour durations on the supposition that subsequent days will mirror the 24-hour period. However, this is not always true. The initial conditions (i.e. tank levels and pump operation) tend to distort the results somewhat and only by running at least two days can a model user be sure that subsequent days will be like the first day. Some problems (especially those dealing with tank refilling) may not show up until the second or third day.

Time Step Size

The time step size is a site specific parameter which depends on the natural fluctuations in the distribution system. If pumps are cycling every 20 minutes then a 10 minute time step is needed. If the pumps are cycling roughly every three hours, then an hour time step is acceptable. If the system runs steadily with only minor fluctuations in demand, it may be possible to use 3 hour time steps.

Long durations with small time steps and large systems without much skeletonization tend to result in somewhat long run times. It is important that the model user have adequate computer power to run the model effectively.

Batch Runs

Recent advances in models which make it possible to run several scenarios at once and compare the results in a single graph have made using EPS models easier than ever before.

The time step size is a site specific parameter that depends on the natural fluctuations in the distribution system.

What to Look for in Output

Because they calculate information at each time step for every node, pipe, pump, tank, and valve, EPS models produce a huge set of numbers. Computers are great for crunching numbers; however, reviewing these numbers in tabular form for a real system is a daunting if not impossible task. Computer generated graphics are the only way to quickly get a handle on what a given run means.

Early pipe network models had either no graphics at all or rudimentary graphics that were not user friendly. In order to graphically review the results, some model users would try to export data to other software. With recent advances through models such as WaterCAD® and Cybernet®, viewing EPS results has become a quick easy step in the modeling process. The ability of models to plot the results of several runs (scenarios) on a single graph has become an especially valuable tool for design comparisons.

The following sections show model results and include discussions on what the user should look for in the graphical output.

Evaluating Pumping Capacity

Usually the best indicator of how a system is performing is a graph of tank level vs. time. Such a graph can provide insights on whether the system will work when placed in service. Figure 1-13 shows the fluctuations in tank water level for a system with three alternative pumps for a peak day demand. The curve labeled "Good Pump" shows how the tank level would fluctuate if the pump were matched well with the demands. The pump runs steadily and tank levels stay in the 10 ft. range from 290 ft. to 300 ft. set by the modeler.

The curve labeled "Large Pump" shows a pump with excess capacity such that it cycles on and off a few times, filling up the tank in a few hours and then remaining off for the rest of the day. Such a pump would be good if the source (e.g. well, treatment plant, clearwell) could keep up with the pump discharge.

The curve labeled "Small Pump" shows what would happen with an undersized pump. Only by letting the water level drop to a point where its discharge matched the demand would it work. Because of the way in which pump curves drop off steeply, a pump does not need to be undersized greatly to cause a shortfall in supply.

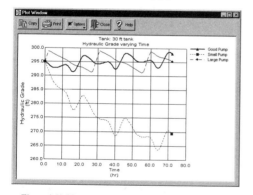

Figure 1-13: Tank level vs. time for 3 alternative pumps

Evaluating Piping Capacity

A similar plot of tank level vs. time for several different main sizes feeding the tank is shown in Figure 1-14. A 10 in. pipe can keep tank levels above the target of 290 ft. A 12 in. pipe only slightly improves capacity because once the velocity becomes small, increasing pipe size makes little difference. However, decreasing the pipe size to 8 in. results in inadequate tank filling rates and excessive draining rates.

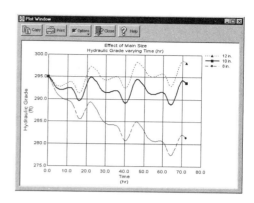

Figure 1-14: Tank level vs. time for 3 different main sizes

Tank Volume

Figure 1-15 shows how tanks with different volumes perform in EPS models. The 30 ft. diameter tank shows a reasonable diurnal fluctuation. The 20 ft. tank shows more cycling of the pumps feeding the system, but may still be satisfactory. However, the 10 ft. diameter tank results in much more cycling and thus the system can not keep up with peak demands during several hours (15, 39, and 64) of the three days run (only first 40 hours are shown).

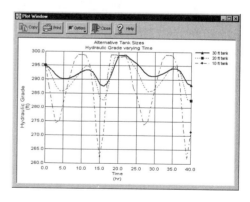

Figure 1-15: Performance of different volume tanks in an EPS simulation

Tank Elevation

While much of the work in determining the overflow elevation for a tank can be done with steady state models, EPS runs can also provide some insights. Figure 1-16 shows three tanks with

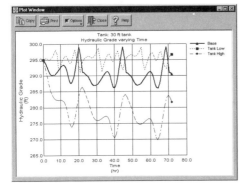

Figure 1-16: Determining tank overflow elevations with an EPS simulation

overflow at 300 ft. In the case labeled "tank low," the tank is at too low of an elevation for the system and pumps. In this case the tank fills quickly and shuts off the pumps. As a result, the pressure drops, and the pumps have to keep cycling to keep the tanks in the desirable range. For "tank high," the tank is at too high of an elevation and thus it is difficult to keep the tank water level in the desired range of 290 to 300 ft. without over pressurizing at least some of the system. Although it is always possible to change pumps and controls to work with a tank at an incorrect elevation, there will be problems providing service to customers at high or low elevations.

Low Pressure

There are always a few locations in any pressure zone that have problems with low pressure. EPS model output can help the user distinguish between low pressures due to elevations and those due to excessive head loss. In the first case the

solution may be pumping to a new zone, pressure reducing valve (PRV) adjustments, or moving the customers to an adjacent higher pressure zone. In the second, more piping capacity, opening a throttled valve, or adding a tank near the customer is needed.

Figure 1-17 shows that customers at a high elevation will have pressure graphs that are consistently low. On the other hand, customers with low pressures due to inadequate piping capacity will have graphs with low pressure only during peak demand periods.

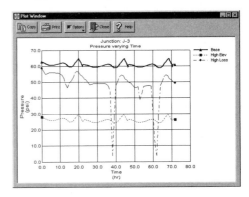

Figure 1-17: Identifying low pressure areas with an EPS simulation

PRV Pressures and Flows

The graph of a downstream pressure at a properly operating PRV is fairly dull, a straight line with constant pressure. However, a plot of flow through the PRV can provide information on flow rates that is generally not available to the utility (because flow is not measured through most PRV's).

An even more interesting situation corresponds to a PRV that is a backup feed (sometimes called a "sleeper" PRV) to a pressure zone. The model can calculate when it is operational and produce a graph of flow vs. time as in Figure 1-18 or pressure vs. time as in Figure 1-19. Figure 1-19 should match the results of a pressure chart on the downstream side of the PRV. When the PRV is closed, the pressure is dictated by other sources. When the PRV is in operation, the pressure is a constant at the PRV setting.

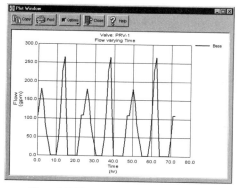

Figure 1-18: Flow vs. time for a "sleeper valve"

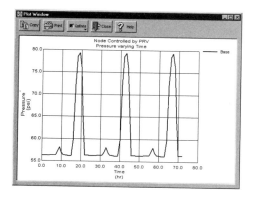

Figure 1-19: Pressure vs. time for a "sleeper valve"

fluctuations in a system which tries to keep its tanks full. Figure 1-21 shows the fluctuations in a pump discharge in an attempt to keep the tank full. A larger span between "pump on" and "pump off" settings will reduce the period of these fluctuations.

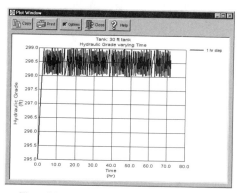

Figure 1-20: Fluctuation in water level when pumps attempt to keep the tank full

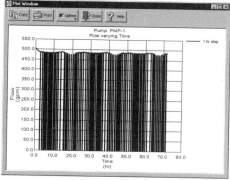

Figure 1-21: Fluctuations in pump discharge working to keep the tank full

Pump Controls

Some water companies like to keep their tanks full such that whenever the water level drops as much as a foot from the top, they turn pumps on. This can result in poor water quality and excessive pump starts. The impact of establishing "pump on" and "pump off" settings at a tank can be viewed within the model. Figure 1-20 shows the

Tank Off-Line

Occasionally, utilities must take a tank off line for inspection or painting. When this happens a constant speed pump discharging into a dead end system can produce very high pressures during low demand periods. It is a simple matter for the model to predict those pressures as shown in Figure 1-22. (In this example, the pressure would normally be fairly constant at about 74 psi when the tank is on line.) With this information, the water utility can decide whether they need to relieve the pressure while the tank is off-line.

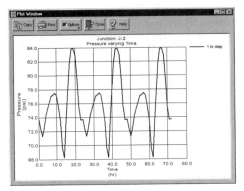

Figure 1-22: High pressures due to offline tank

Fire Events

While a water utility can estimate its fire flows with fire flow tests, it can not check how the system responds for the duration of a two hour, 1000 gpm fire. With an EPS model, the utility can examine how a tank water level would drop during a fire and how it would refill after the fire. In Figure 1-23, the tank barely stays above its 260 ft bottom during a fire from hour two to hour four. It takes until

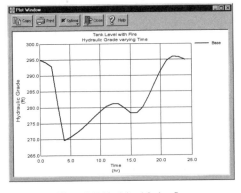

Figure 1-23: Tank level during fire

nearly hour 20 for the tank level to recover. If the fire had gone on for three hours, instead of two, the tank would have drained. This also could have been simulated with the model. Figure 1-24 shows how the pump discharge increases during and after the fire due to the demand of the fire and the low tank level which results in the pump moving further out on its curve. If the pump runs too far out on its curve, it may trip the motor and shut down.

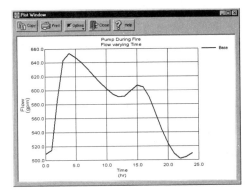

Figure 1-24: Pump discharge during fire

Pipe Breaks

A pipe break is similar to a fire in that there is a large flow for several hours while the break is isolated and during that time the tank is counted on to provide the extra water. However, in the case of a fire the tank begins to refill immediately after the fire, while in the case of a break, there is an initial time (hours 2 to 4 in Figure 1-25) where the leakage is very high (500 gpm) followed by 10 hours where flows are restricted in an important main while the break is repaired. Only after the break is repaired and the pipe is placed back in service will the tank recover (after hour 15).

Impact of Time Step Size

Sometimes the model does not accurately represent what would occur in the field. One such situation occurs when there are too few time steps

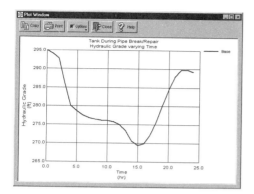

Figure 1-25: Tank level during pipe break

to capture variations in system behavior. Figure 1-26 shows the pump discharge rate with a pump that cycles every few hours. One hour time steps fairly accurately reflect pump behavior while two hour steps miss some of the variations. Six hour time steps present a completely misleading picture of what is happening in the system. Time steps need to be appropriately sized in order to capture what is happening in the system.

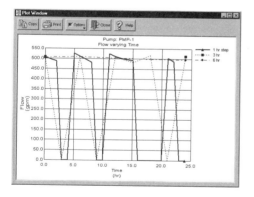

Figure 1-26: Impact of time step size

Tank Level Oscillations

If tanks located near one another have very different water levels at the start of a simulation, the model can make the water appear to slosh back and forth between the tanks even though this

would not occur in the real system. The model will be unstable even though, in the real system, friction would prevent this from occurring. Figure 1-27 shows the type of fluctuations that should make the user cautious. This situation should be avoided by starting adjacent tanks off with similar water levels. In this example there was a 40 ft. difference between the water levels of the two tanks at the start of the EPS.

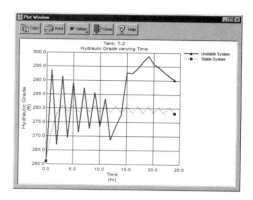

Figure 1-27: Tank level oscillations

Summary

Software such as Cybernet® and WaterCAD® make EPS models easy enough to use that they can be applied to a wide variety of situations. In order to take full advantage of this capability, the user must know what to look for in the results.

Author: Thomas Walski, Ph.D., PE

Modeling Scenarios with Ease

Complete your projects faster and improve your bottom line.

Haestad Methods' scenario management feature is available in such top-of-the-line numerical models as Cybernet®, WaterCAD®, and StormCAD®. This feature can dramatically increase your productivity in the "what-if…" areas of modeling, including calibration, operations analysis, and planning.

By investing a little time now to understand scenario management, you can avoid unnecessary editing and data duplication. Take advantage of scenario management to get a lot more out of your model – with much less work and expense.

Before Haestad Methods: Manual Scenarios

Let's begin by understanding the approaches that have historically been used to attempt "what-if" analyses. Traditionally, there have only been two possible ways of analyzing the effects of change on a software model (Figure 1-28):

• Change the model, recalculate, and review the results.

• Create a copy of the model, edit that copy, calculate, and review the results.

Although either of these methods may be adequate for a relatively small system, the data duplication, editing, and re-editing becomes very time-consuming and error-prone as the size of the system, and the number of possible conditions, increase. Additionally, comparing conditions requires manual data manipulation, because all output needs to be stored in physically separate data files.

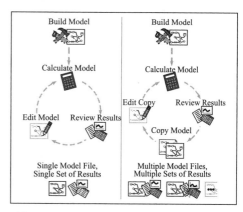

Figure 1-28: Before Haestad Methods: manual scenarios

With Haestad Methods: Self-Contained Scenarios

Effective scenario management tools need to meet these objectives:

- Minimize the number of project files the modeler needs to maintain (one, ideally)

- Maximize the usefulness of scenarios through easy access to input and output data, direct comparisons, etc.

- Maximize the number of scenarios the user can simulate by mixing and matching data from existing scenarios (no new data)

- Minimize the amount of data that needs to be duplicated to consider conditions that have a lot in common.

The scenario management feature developed by Haestad Methods successfully meets all of these objectives. A single project file enables the modeler to generate an unlimited number of "what-if" conditions, edit only the data that needs to be changed, and quickly generate direct comparisons of input and results for desired scenarios.

The Scenario Cycle

The process of working with scenarios is similar to the process of manually copying and editing data, but without the disadvantages of data duplication and troublesome file management (Figure 1-29). This process allows the user to cycle through any number of changes to the model, without fear of overwriting critical data or duplicating important information. Of course, it is possible to directly change data for any scenario, but an "audit trail" of scenarios can be useful for retracing the steps of a calibration series or for understanding a group of master plan updates.

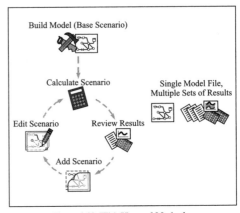

Figure 1-29: With Haestad Methods: self-contained scenarios

Scenario Anatomy: Attributes and Alternatives

Before we explore scenario management further, let's define a few key terms:

Attribute. An attribute is a fundamental property of an object, and is often a single numeric quantity. For example, the attributes of a pipe include diameter, length, and roughness.

Alternative: An alternative holds a family of related attributes, so that pieces of data that you are most likely to change together are grouped for easy referencing and editing. For example, a demand alternative groups baseline loads and patterns for the network's junction nodes.

Scenario: A scenario has a list of referenced alternatives (which hold the attributes) and combines these alternatives to form an overall set of system conditions that can be analyzed. This referencing of alternatives enables the user to easily generate system conditions that mix and match groups of data that have been previously created. Note that scenarios don't actually hold any attribute data – the referenced alternatives do.

A Familiar Parallel

Although the structure of scenarios may seem a bit difficult at first, anyone who has eaten at a restaurant should be able to relate fairly easily. A meal (scenario) is comprised of several courses (alternatives), which might include a salad, an entrée, and a dessert. Each course has its own attributes – for example, the entrée may have a meat, a vegetable, and a starch. Examining the choices, we could present a menu as in Figure 1-30.

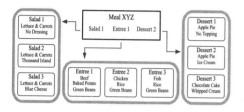

Figure 1-30: A restaurant meal "scenario"

The restaurant doesn't have to create a new recipe for every possible meal (combination of courses) that could be ordered – they can just assemble any meal based on what the customer orders for each alternative course. Salad 1, Entrée 1, and Dessert 2 might then be combined to define a complete meal.

Generalizing this concept (Figure 1-31), we see that any scenario simply references one alternative from each category to create a "big picture" that can be analyzed. Note that different types of alternatives may have different numbers and types of attributes, and any category can have an unlimited number of alternatives to choose from.

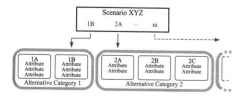

Figure 1-31: Generic scenario anatomy

Scenario Behavior: Inheritance

The separation of scenarios into distinct alternatives (groups of data) meets one of the basic goals of scenario management: maximizing the number of scenarios the user can develop by mixing and matching existing alternatives (no new data). Two other primary goals have also been addressed: a single project file is used, and easy access to input data and calculated results is provided in numerous formats through the intuitive graphical interface.

But what about the other objective: minimizing the amount of data that needs to be duplicated to consider conditions that have a lot of common input? Surely an entire set of junction demands shouldn't be re-specified if only one or two change?

The solution is a familiar concept to most people: *inheritance.*

A child inherits characteristics from a parent. In the natural world, this may include such traits as eye-color, hair color, bone structure, etc. Two significant differences between the genetic inheritance that most of us know and the way inheritance is implemented in software are:

• Overriding inheritance

• Dynamic inheritance

Overriding Inheritance

Overriding inheritance is the software equivalent of cosmetics. A child can override inherited characteristics at any time by specifying a new value for that characteristic. These overriding values do not affect the parent, and are therefore considered "local" to the child. Local values can also be removed at any time, reverting the characteristic to its inherited state. The child has no choice in the value of his inherited attributes, only in local attributes.

For example, suppose a child has inherited the attribute of blue eyes from his parent. Now the child puts on a pair of green-tinted contact lenses to hide his natural eye color. When the contact lenses are on, we say his natural eye color is "overridden" locally, and his eye color is green. When the child removes the tinted lenses, his eye color instantly reverts to blue, as inherited from his parent.

Dynamic Inheritance

Dynamic inheritance does not have a parallel in the genetic world. When a parent's characteristic is changed, existing children also reflect the change. Using the eye-color example from above, this would be the equivalent of the parent changing eye color from blue to brown, and the children's eyes instantly inheriting the brown color also. Of course, if the child has already overridden a characteristic locally, as with the green lenses, his eyes will remain green until the lenses are removed (at which point his eye color will revert to the inherited color, now brown).

This dynamic inheritance has remarkable benefits for applying wide-scale changes to a model, fixing an error, and so on. If rippling changes are not desired, the child can override all of the parent's values, or a copy of the parent can be made instead of a child.

When are values local, and when are they inherited?

Any **changes** that are made to the model belong to the currently active scenario (and the alternatives that it references). If that alternative happens to

have children, those children will inherit the changes unless they have also specifically overridden that attribute. Figure 1-32 demonstrates the effects of a change to a mid-level alternative (inherited values are shown as gray text, local values are shown as black text):

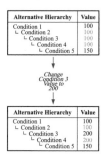

Figure 1-32: A mid-level hierarchy alternative change

Minimizing Effort through Attribute Inheritance

Inheritance has an application every time you hear the phrase "just like x except for y". Rather than specifying all of the data from x again to form this new condition, we can simply create a child from x and change y appropriately. Now we have both conditions, with no duplicated effort.

We can even apply this inheritance to our restaurant analogy, as shown in Figure 1-33, 1-34, and 1-35 (inherited values are shown as gray text, local values are shown as black text):

Salad Alternative Hierarchy	Attribute: Vegetables	Attribute: Dressing
Salad 1	Lettuce & Carrots	No Dressing
Salad 2	Lettuce & Carrots	Thousand Island
Salad 3	Lettuce & Carrots	Blue Cheese

Figure 1-33

- "Salad 2 is just like Salad 1, except for the dressing."

- "Salad 3 is just like Salad 1, except for the dressing."

- Note that Salad 3 could inherit from Salad 2, if we prefer: "Salad 3 is just like Salad 2, except for the dressing."

Entree Alternative Hierarchy	Attribute: Meat	Attribute: Starch	Attribute: Vegetable
Entree 1	Beef	Baked Potato	Green Beans
└ Entree 2	Chicken	Rice	Green Beans
└ Entree 3	Fish	Rice	Green Beans

Figure 1-34

- "Entrée 2 is just like Entrée 1, except for the meat and the starch."

- "Entrée 3 is just like Entrée 2, except for the meat."

- Note that if the vegetable of the day changes (say from green beans to peas), only Entrée 1 needs to be updated, and the other entrées will be automatically inherit the vegetable a attribute of "Peas" instead of "Green Beans."

Dessert Alternative Hierarchy	Attribute: Bakery Item	Attribute: Topping
Dessert 1	Apple Pie	No Topping
└ Dessert 2	Apple Pie	Ice Cream
Dessert 3	Chocolate Cake	Whipped Cream

Figure 1-35

- "Dessert 2 is just like Dessert 1, except for the topping"

- Note that Dessert 3 has nothing in common with the other desserts, so it can be created as a "root" or "base" alternative – it does not inherit its attribute data from any other alternative.

Minimizing Effort through Scenario Inheritance

Just as a child alternative can inherit attributes from its parent, a child scenario can inherit which alternatives it references from its parent. This is essentially still the phrase "just like x except for y", but on a larger scale.

Carrying through our meal example, consider a situation where you go out to dinner with three friends. The first friend places his order, and the second friend orders the same thing except for the dessert. The third friend orders something totally different, and you order the same meal as hers except for the salad.

The four meal "scenarios" could then be presented as shown in Figure 1-36 (inherited values are shown as gray text, local values are shown as black text):

Meal Scenario Hierarchy	Salad Alternative	Entree Alternative	Dessert Alternative
Meal 1	Salad 1	Entree 2	Dessert 3
└ Meal 2	Salad 1	Entree 2	Dessert 1
Meal 3	Salad 3	Entree 3	Dessert 2
└ Meal 4	Salad 2	Entree 3	Dessert 2

Figure 1-36

- "Meal 2 is just like Meal 1, except for the dessert." (The salad and entrée alternatives are inherited from Meal 1)

- "Meal 3 is nothing like Meal 1 or Meal 2" (A totally new "base" or "root" is created)

- "Meal 4 is just like Meal 3, except for the salad." (The entrée and dessert alternatives are inherited from Meal 3).

A Water Distribution Example

Let's consider a fairly simple water distribution system: a single reservoir supplies water by gravity to three junction nodes (Figure 1-37).

Although true water distribution scenarios include such alternative categories as initial settings, operational controls, water quality, and fire flow, we are going to focus on the two most commonly changed sets of alternatives: demands and physical properties. Within these alternatives, we are going to concentrate on junction baseline demands and pipe diameters.

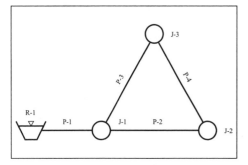

Figure 1-37: Example water distribution system

Building the Model (Average Day Conditions)

During model construction, probably only one alternative from each category is going to be considered. This model is built with average demand calculations and preliminary pipe diameter estimates. At this point we can name our scenario and alternatives, and the hierarchies look like Figure 1-38 (showing only the items of interest).

Demand Alternative Hierarchy	J-1	J-2	J-3
Average Day	100 gpm	500 gpm	100 gpm

Physical Alternative Hierarchy	P-1	P-2	P-3	P-4
Preliminary Pipes	8 inches	6 inches	6 inches	6 inches

Scenario Hierarchy	Demand Alternative	Physical Alternative
Avg. Day	Average Day	Preliminary Pipes

Figure 1-38

Analyzing Different Demands (Maximum Day Conditions)

The local planning board also requires analysis of maximum day demands, so a new demand alternative is required. No variation in demand is

expected at J-2, which is an industrial site. As a result, the new demand alternative can inherit J-2's demand from "Average Day" while the other two demands are overridden (Figure 1-39).

Demand Alternative Hierarchy	J-1	J-2	J-3
Average Day	100 gpm	500 gpm	100 gpm
└ Maximum Day	200 gpm	500 gpm	200 gpm

Figure 1-39

Now we can create a child scenario from "Avg. Day" that inherits the physical alternative, but overrides the selected demand alternative. As a result, we get the following scenario hierarchy (Figure 1-40).

Scenario Hierarchy	Demand Alternative	Physical Alternative
Avg. Day	Average Day	Preliminary Pipes
└ Max. Day	Maximum Day	Preliminary Pipes

Figure 1-40

Since no physical data (pipe diameters) have been changed, the physical alternative hierarchy remains the same as before.

Another Set of Demands (Peak Hour Conditions)

Based on pressure requirements, the system is adequate to supply maximum day demands. Another local regulation requires analysis of peak hour demands, with slightly lower allowable pressures. Since the peak hour demands also share the industrial load from the "Average Day" condition, let's inherit "Peak Hour" from "Average Day". In this instance, "Peak Hour" could inherit just as easily from "Maximum Day" (Figure 1-41).

Demand Alternative Hierarchy	J-1	J-2	J-3
Average Day	100 gpm	500 gpm	100 gpm
├ Maximum Day	200 gpm	500 gpm	200 gpm
└ Peak Hour	250 gpm	500 gpm	250 gpm

Figure 1-41

Another scenario is also created to reference these new demands, as shown in Figure 1-42. Note again that we did not change any physical data, so the physical alternatives remain the same.

Scenario Hierarchy	Demand Alternative	Physical Alternative
Avg. Day	Average Day	Preliminary Pipes
├ Max. Day	Maximum Day	Preliminary Pipes
└ Peak	Peak Hour	Preliminary Pipes

Figure 1-42

Correcting an Error

This analysis also results in acceptable pressures... until it is discovered that the industrial demand is not actually 500 gpm – it should be 1,500 gpm! Because of the inheritance within the demand alternatives, however, only the "Average Day" demand for J-2 needs to be updated (and the changes will ripple through the children). After the single change is made, the demand hierarchy is as shown in Figure 1-43.

Demand Alternative Hierarchy	J-1	J-2	J-3
Average Day	100 gpm	*1,500 gpm*	100 gpm
├ Maximum Day	200 gpm	*1,500 gpm*	200 gpm
└ Peak Hour	250 gpm	*1,500 gpm*	250 gpm

Figure 1-43

Notice that no changes need to be made to the scenarios to reflect these corrections. The three scenarios can now be calculated as a batch to update the results.

When these results are reviewed, it is determined that the system does not have the ability to adequately supply the system as it was originally thought – the pressure at J-2 is too low under peak hour demand conditions.

Analyzing Improvement Suggestions

To counter the headloss from the increased demand load, two possible improvements are suggested:

- A much larger diameter is proposed for P-1 (the pipe from the reservoir). This physical alternative is created as a child of the "Preliminary Pipes" alternative, inheriting all the diameters except P-1's, which is overridden.

- Slightly larger diameters are proposed for all pipes. Since there are no commonalties between this recommendation and either of the other physical alternatives, this can be created as a base (root) alternative.

These changes are then incorporated to arrive at the following hierarchies (Figure 1-44):

Physical Alternative Hierarchy	P-1	P-2	P-3	P-4
Preliminary Pipes	8 inches	6 inches	6 inches	6 inches
└ *Larger P-1*	*18 inches*	6 inches	6 inches	6 inches
Larger All Pipes	*12 inches*	*12 inches*	*12 inches*	*12 inches*

Scenario Hierarchy	Demand Alternative	Physical Alternative
Avg. Day	Average Day	Preliminary Pipes
├ Max. Day	Maximum Day	Preliminary Pipes
└ Peak	Peak Hour	Preliminary Pipes
├ *Peak, Big P-1*	Peak Hour	*Larger P-1*
└ *Peak, All Big Pipes*	Peak Hour	*Larger All Pipes*

Figure 1-44

This time, the demand alternative hierarchy remains the same since no demands were changed. The two new scenarios ("Peak, Big P-1", "Peak, All Big Pipes") can be batch run to provide results for these proposed improvements.

Next, features like Scenario Comparison Annotation (from the Scenario Manager) and comparison graphs (for extended period simulations, from the element editor dialogs) can be used to directly determine which proposal results in the most improved pressures.

Finalizing the Project

It is decided that enlarging P-1 is the optimum solution, so new scenarios are created to check the results for average day and maximum day demands (Figure 1-45). Notice that this step does not require handling any new data – all of the information we want to model is present in the alternatives we already have!

Scenario Hierarchy	Demand Alternative	Physical Alternative
Average. Day	Average Day	Preliminary Pipes
├ Max. Day	Maximum Day	Preliminary Pipes
└ *Max. Day, Big P-1*	Maximum Day	*Larger P-1*
├ Peak	Peak Hour	Preliminary Pipes
├ Peak, Big P-1	Peak Hour	Larger P-1
└ Peak, All Big Pipes	Peak Hour	Larger All Pipes
└ *Avg. Day, Big P-1*	Average Day	*Larger P-1*

Figure 1-45

Also note that it would be equally effective in this case to inherit the "Avg. Day, Big P-1" scenario from "Avg. Day" (changing the physical alternative) or to inherit from "Peak, Big P-1" (changing the demand alternative). Likewise, "Max. Day, Big P-1" could inherit from either "Max. Day" or "Peak, Big P-1".

Neither the demand nor physical alternative hierarchies were changed in order to run the last set of scenarios, so they remain as they were (Figure 1-46).

Demand Alternative Hierarchy	J-1	J-2	J-3
Average Day	100 gpm	1,500 gpm	100 gpm
├ Maximum Day	200 gpm	1,500 gpm	200 gpm
└ Peak Hour	250 gpm	1,500 gpm	250 gpm

Physical Alternative Hierarchy	P-1	P-2	P-3	P-4
Preliminary Pipes	8 inches	6 inches	6 inches	6 inches
└ Larger P-1	18 inches	6 inches	6 inches	6 inches
Larger All Pipes	12 inches	12 inches	12 inches	12 inches

Figure 1-46

Summary

In contrast to the old manual methods of scenario management (editing or copying data) automated scenario management using inheritance gives you significant advantages:

- A single project file makes it possible to generate an unlimited number of "what-if…" conditions without becoming overwhelmed with numerous modeling files and separate results.

- Because the software maintains the data for all the scenarios in a single project, it can provide you with powerful automated tools for directly comparing scenario results. Any set of results is immediately available at any time.

- The Scenario/Alternative relationship empowers you to mix and match groups of data from existing scenarios without having to re-declare any data at all.

- With inheritance, you do not have to re-enter data if it remains unchanged in a new alternative or scenario (avoiding redundant copies of the same data). Inheritance also enables you to correct a data input error in a parent scenario and automatically update the corrected attribute in all the child scenarios.

These advantages, while obvious, may not seem compelling for small projects. It is as projects grow to hundreds or thousands of network elements that the advantages of true scenario inheritance become clear. On a large project, being able to maintain a collection of base and modified alternatives – accurately and efficiently – can be the difference between evaluating optional improvements and being forced to ignore them.

In Conclusion

Haestad Methods' scenario management feature gives you a powerful tool for modeling real-world engineering scenarios when analyzing system response to different demands, reviewing the impacts of future growth, and iterating to find the least expensive design. That means you will be able to finish your projects faster, spend less money, and improve your bottom line.

Coauthors: Gregg A. Herrin & Darrow Kirkpatrick

Performing an Automated Fire Flow Analysis

The automated fire flow analysis is a powerful tool that any hydraulic network modeler should find easy to add to their repertoire.

Most communities choose to size their water distribution system such that it will provide sufficient fire protection services. Thus, the evaluation of water distribution system performance under fire flow conditions is one of the more common applications of network hydraulic models. Performing a fire flow test on every hydrant in an actual system would be prohibitively expensive and disruptive. Fortunately, products such as WaterCAD® and Cybernet® are available to the engineer to model and automatically test the system. Once the theory and parameters behind a fire flow analysis are understood it is very easy to implement such simulations using these programs.

...avoid having to perform the hundreds or even thousands of steady state simulations required to adequately test a large system.

With the proper parameters these products will perform an automated fire flow simulation to provide the engineer with the available fire flow at every node in a network. The engineer can thus avoid having to perform the hundreds or even thousands of steady state simulations required to adequately test a large system. The automated fire flow simulation is extremely useful, very easy to use, and can save the engineer a tremendous amount of time.

Common Fire Flow Methods

The goal of the fire flow analysis is to ensure that the system design will support enough flow to control a fire while maintaining a minimum residual pressure in the system. The first question that arises is how much flow is needed to control a fire? There are three common methods used to estimate the fire flow requirement for a particular structure. They were developed by:

- the Insurance Services Office (ISO),

- Iowa State University (ISU), and

- the Illinois Institute of Technology Research Institute (IITRI).

The ISO method calculates the design fire flow based on the type of construction, square footage, influence of the occupancy, exposure of neighboring buildings, and the ability of the fire to spread within the building. The ISU method uses only the volume of the space within the building to calculate the fire flow, but it assumes that the entire space is burning. The IITRI method determines the needed fire flow based on the area of the fire and whether or not the building is residential. Table 1-1 shows a comparison of the required fire flows calculated for a one story, non-residential building of ordinary construction for these three methods. For further discussion and more detail on each of these methods see the AWWA Manual M31 (AWWA, 1992) entitled "Distribution System Requirements for Fire Protection."

Method	Fireflows
ISO	1000 gpm
ISU	1000 gpm
IITRI	2900 gpm

Table 1-1: Comparison of required fire flows

For most water distribution systems the minimum allowable fire flow is 500 gpm and the expected upper limit is about 3,500 gpm (AWWA Manual M31, 1992). Usually the required fire flow is added to the maximum daily demand to determine the appropriate design flow for the fire flow test. A sprinkler system in a building often decreases the amount of required fire flow, but the modeler must remember to include the flow to the sprinkler system in the design fire flow. When the design fire flow is applied to each corresponding hydrant, the pressure in the system should not violate any of the pressure constraints set for the system.

Manual Fire Flow Test

The fire flow test can be performed manually. One way to do this is by manually adding the fire flow to a node in the system and then running the model. After the model has run, the engineer must check that none of the pressure constraints are violated. This can be accomplished by first checking the residual pressure. If this is adequate then the user can filter out the nodes that exceeded the minimum pressure constraints. This allows the user to quickly determine if there are any problem nodes. This process is then repeated for every node in the system that needs to be tested. For a large system this is a tedious time consuming process. Fortunately, the engineer can employ the automated fire flow test in WaterCAD® or Cybernet® to automate this process and save an enormous amount of time.

Automated Fire Flow Analysis

The automated fire flow analysis provides the user with the flexibility to test a single node, a group of nodes, or all the nodes in the system. At each of the nodes specified by the user the computer model iteratively assigns a demand. Often this is added to the maximum daily demand. If the base demand is significantly less than the maximum demand then the engineer will want to globally edit the base demand and apply a factor that will set it about equal to the maximum demand.

The computer model uses the constraints entered by the user to define boundaries for the possible fire flows that must be tested. If the available fire flow lies outside this bounded set of values then the fire flow result computed by the model defaults to one of the boundary values. If the fire flow is within this bounded set then the model iteratively divides this range until it converges on a solution or reaches the maximum number of iterations.

Automated Fire Flow Example

In order to make it easy to understand all the parameters involved in an automated fire flow analysis and how they can be entered in a model, the following example presents the step by step process involved in performing such an analysis. Figure 1-47 is the simple model that will be used in

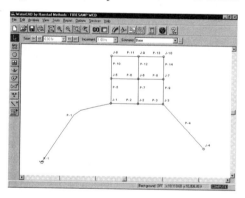

Figure 1-47: Water distribution network

this example. Since this model only contains the average daily demands we may need to account for the fact that the maximum daily demands will be larger. By globally editing the demands that are placed at each junction, all demands can be scaled up by a factor of 1.5. This is a fairly typical value to use when you don't have any specific data on past consumption (AWWA, 1992). If you do have data

on past consumption then you should select a factor that will bring the base demand close to the maximum demand level. In our case, a *Global Edit* can be performed on the demands in the junction tabular report. This will allow us to either add to, subtract from, multiply, or divide all demands by a constant amount (see Figure 1-48).

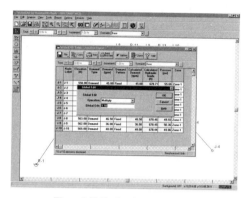

Figure 1-48: Performing a global edit

To determine the parameters that will apply for this fire flow alternative, click on the *Analysis* menu and select the *Alternative Manager* option. In the window that pops up, select the *Fire Flow Tab* and highlight the fire flow alternative that you wish to edit by clicking on it. In our case there is only one fire flow alternative so it is already highlighted. Now click the edit button to enter the various constraints. This brings up the window shown in Figure 1-49, which is one of the places where the parameters regarding the fire flow analysis can be entered and edited.

There are a number of different fields in this window and it is important that the modeler have an in depth understanding of each one in order to properly perform a fire flow test. The fields are organized into four different sections: flow constraints, selection set, pressure constraints and a table summarizing the information.

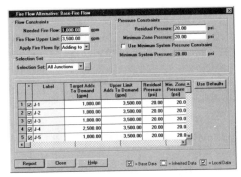

Figure 1-49: Entering and editing fire flow parameters

Flow Constraints

The *Flow Constraints* section has three fields, the first of which is the *Needed Fire Flow*. This is the minimum amount of fire flow that any junction being tested must be able to supply. For our model we will set this number to 1000 gpm.

Under the needed fire flow is the field to enter the *Fire Flow Upper Limit*. This is the maximum amount of fire flow that the model will try to withdraw from any junction. This limit prevents the model from testing the impractical high values that could result if the simulated fire flow came off a large diameter high capacity pipe such as a trunk line. For our model, we will set this value to 3500 gpm which is the upper limit that most utilities should expect to provide (AWWA M31, 1992).

In the next drop down list entitled *Apply Fire Flows By* the user can indicate whether to replace the baseline demand with the fire flow or add the fire flow to the baseline demand. In our model we will choose to add the fire flow demand to the baseline. This ensures that the system will provide the expected fire flow even if the other users connected to a particular junction are still using water.

Selection Set

Under the *Flow Constraints* section is the *Selection Set*. This section has one field which allows the user to specify the working set of junctions to be analyzed. In our model we will test *All Junctions* in the system. If only a subset of the junctions needs to be tested then the user should choose the *Subset of Junctions* option. Then you can click on the ellipsis button next to the drop down box to select the junctions that need to be tested.

Pressure Constraints

Adjacent to the *Flow Constraints* and *Selection Set* sections is the *Pressure Constraints* section. The first field in this section is for the *Residual Pressure*. This is the minimum pressure that is allowed to occur at the fire flow withdrawal location. The model is constrained so that the pressure at the withdrawal location does not fall below this point. In our model we will set this to the typical value of 20 psi.

The field under the *Residual Pressure* is the *Minimum Zone Pressure*. This is the minimum pressure that can occur at any other junction within the same zone as the junction being tested. Zones are used to split the system up into different pressure areas. For example, a point on the suction side of a pump will often have a pressure much lower then the rest of the system. If this causes the fire flow pressure constraints to be violated then this point can be put into another pressure zone. This way it will not violate the minimum zone pressure requirement. In our example, we will set the minimum zone pressure to 20 psi.

The next field, *Minimum System Pressure*, is optional. The minimum system pressure is the minimum pressure allowed to occur at any junction in the entire system. This constraint applies regardless of the zone boundaries in the system. This allows the user to ensure that the pressures in pressure zones other than the one being tested do not fall below a minimum level due to the withdrawal of fireflow. To set the minimum system pressure, check the box next to the label *Use Minimum System Pressure Constraint*. Then enter the minimum system pressure in the field below this.

Summary Table

The last item in the window is a table which lists the set of junctions that are to be tested. The data that was entered into the fields above is used as the default values for the fire flow constraints for each of these junctions. If a junction has different constraints than those in the above fields, you can override the default values in this table.

For example, junction J-4 in the model occurs at an industrial site. Because of this we want to make sure that we have more fire flow at this location then the amount we specified for all the other junctions. We can change the data for this one junction in the summary table. To do this we scroll down to junction J-4, click on the value in the *Target Adds to Demand* column, and change the value from 1000 to 2500. Now junction J-4 has a minimum fire flow of 2500 gpm while all the other junctions have a minimum fire flow of 1000 gpm. Any other values in the table can be edited in a similar fashion.

Once all the data has been entered in the *Fire Flow Alternative* window the model can be run to see if the system passes the fire flow test. In order to run the fire flow analysis, close the alternative windows to get to the main window and click the GO button at the top of the screen to bring up the window shown in Figure 1-50. Make sure that the model is set to run a *Steady State* analysis and that there is a check mark next to the *Fire Flow Analysis* label in the analysis section of the window.

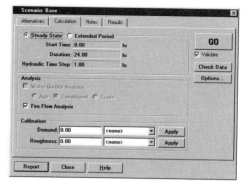

Figure 1-50: Preparing run-time options

Press the GO button to run the model and the results screen should pop up. If the run is successful, there will be a green light indicating success. Open the fire flow report by clicking on *Report* in the menu and then selecting *Tabular Reports* and *Fire Flow* report from that menu. This should open a window like Figure 1-51. The engineer can see if the system passed the fire flow test by verifying that all the junctions have a check mark in the boxes in the column labeled *Satisfies Fire Flow Constraints*. Any junction that does not have a check in the box did not pass the fire flow test. Note that junction J-4 has an available fire flow of 2,364.5 gpm which is less than the required 2,500 gpm.

For larger models, the modeler can utilize the built in sort and filter features to quickly locate the failure node. In addition to letting the user know if the junction could supply the fire flow demand it also supplies other information about the fire flow test such as the available fire flow, the total needed fire flow, the residual pressure during the test, the minimum zone pressure, and the node at which the minimum zone pressure occurred.

If the system does not pass the fire flow test then the modeler must use engineering judgement to fix the system. The solution might be as simple as reevaluating the fire flow constraints, the

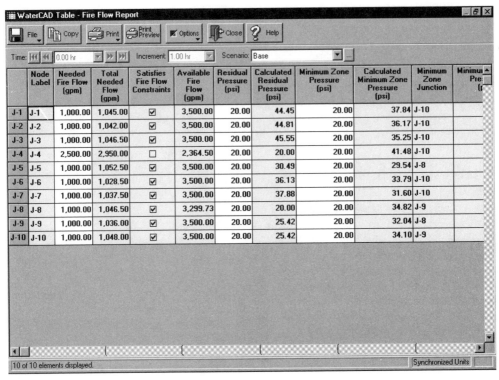

	Node Label	Needed Fire Flow (gpm)	Total Needed Flow (gpm)	Satisfies Fire Flow Constraints	Available Fire Flow (gpm)	Residual Pressure (psi)	Calculated Residual Pressure (psi)	Minimum Zone Pressure (psi)	Calculated Minimum Zone Pressure (psi)	Minimum Zone Junction	Minimu Pre (p
J-1	J-1	1,000.00	1,045.00	☑	3,500.00	20.00	44.45	20.00	37.84	J-10	
J-2	J-2	1,000.00	1,042.00	☑	3,500.00	20.00	44.81	20.00	36.17	J-10	
J-3	J-3	1,000.00	1,046.50	☑	3,500.00	20.00	45.55	20.00	35.25	J-10	
J-4	J-4	2,500.00	2,950.00	☐	2,364.50	20.00	20.00	20.00	41.48	J-10	
J-5	J-5	1,000.00	1,052.50	☑	3,500.00	20.00	30.49	20.00	29.54	J-8	
J-6	J-6	1,000.00	1,028.50	☑	3,500.00	20.00	36.13	20.00	33.79	J-10	
J-7	J-7	1,000.00	1,037.50	☑	3,500.00	20.00	37.88	20.00	31.60	J-10	
J-8	J-8	1,000.00	1,046.50	☑	3,299.73	20.00	20.00	20.00	34.82	J-9	
J-9	J-9	1,000.00	1,036.00	☑	3,500.00	20.00	25.42	20.00	32.04	J-8	
J-10	J-10	1,000.00	1,048.00	☑	3,500.00	20.00	25.42	20.00	34.10	J-9	

10 of 10 elements displayed.   Synchronized Units

Figure 1-51: Fire flow results

assignment of pressure zones, or both. But most of the time these constraints will have been assigned correctly and the modeler will have to propose a design change to meet the demands of the fire suppression system. These changes may include adding another water source, increasing the diameter of some pipes, changing to a larger pump size, or inserting another pump. The final design should solve the immediate problem while giving consideration and staying consistent with the long-term development plans for the system.

In our model the fire flow constraint is not met at junction J-4, so we augment the system by changing the diameter of pipe P-4. We find that if we increase the diameter of pipe P-4 from 10 in. to 12 in. the problem is solved. However, in evaluating the long-term goals of the system we find that this is an area that is expected to grow in the future. Since we need to replace the pipe we might want to consider increasing the diameter of pipe P-4 from 10 in. to 14 in. instead of 12 in. This solution addresses the immediate problem and would be consistent with the long term planning by increasing the water available to the area that is expected to grow in the future. The modeler should ensure that the increased travel time through the pipe resulting from the larger diameter does not adversely effect the water quality in the system.

Observing the results from a run of the fire flow analysis after the diameter of pipe P-14 has been increased shows that the system now meets the demands of the fire suppression system (Figure 1-52).

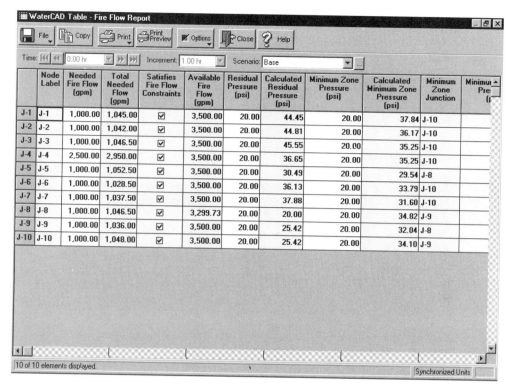

	Node Label	Needed Fire Flow (gpm)	Total Needed Flow (gpm)	Satisfies Fire Flow Constraints	Available Fire Flow (gpm)	Residual Pressure (psi)	Calculated Residual Pressure (psi)	Minimum Zone Pressure (psi)	Calculated Minimum Zone Pressure (psi)	Minimum Zone Junction	Minimum Pre (p
J-1	J-1	1,000.00	1,045.00	☑	3,500.00	20.00	44.45	20.00	37.84	J-10	
J-2	J-2	1,000.00	1,042.00	☑	3,500.00	20.00	44.81	20.00	36.17	J-10	
J-3	J-3	1,000.00	1,046.50	☑	3,500.00	20.00	45.55	20.00	35.25	J-10	
J-4	J-4	2,500.00	2,950.00	☑	3,500.00	20.00	36.65	20.00	35.25	J-10	
J-5	J-5	1,000.00	1,052.50	☑	3,500.00	20.00	30.49	20.00	29.54	J-8	
J-6	J-6	1,000.00	1,028.50	☑	3,500.00	20.00	36.13	20.00	33.79	J-10	
J-7	J-7	1,000.00	1,037.50	☑	3,500.00	20.00	37.88	20.00	31.60	J-10	
J-8	J-8	1,000.00	1,046.50	☑	3,299.73	20.00	20.00	20.00	34.82	J-9	
J-9	J-9	1,000.00	1,036.00	☑	3,500.00	20.00	25.42	20.00	32.04	J-8	
J-10	J-10	1,000.00	1,048.00	☑	3,500.00	20.00	25.42	20.00	34.10	J-9	

Figure 1-52: Fire flow results

Conclusion

Most communities expect their water distribution networks to also function as fire suppression systems. Therefore, the engineer must make sure that these networks can meet the demands placed on them during fire flow conditions. Since it is impractical to physically test every hydrant in the system, a computer simulation is an excellent way for the engineer to evaluate fireflows.

The simplicity and speed of the automated fire flow analysis make it easy for the engineer to rapidly assess the performance of numerous design alternatives and achieve a higher level of confidence that a near optimal solution has been reached. This makes the automated fire flow analysis included in WaterCAD® and Cybernet® a powerful tool for the modeler of hydraulic networks.

Author: Benjamin Wilson

Peaking Factors for Systems with Leakage

Use multipliers to estimate future peak usage.

Most planners project future average day water use and use multipliers (sometimes called "peaking factors") to convert those average day values into maximum day water use or peak hour water use. This process is based on the assumption that certain factors that affect customers' use of water in terms of seasonality and time-of-day use will remain constant in the future.

Unaccounted for water is usually due to leakage, theft, and meter under registration, and in systems where leakage is significant, it tends to be relatively constant over time. As long as leakage remains a small percentage of production over time, multipliers yield a reasonable estimate of future peak usage. However, if leakage is significant, it has the effect of reducing the accuracy of an estimate of future maximum day and peak hour use.

Development of Multipliers

In general, most planners tend to use what will be called "overall" multipliers in which production and demand at each node is multiplied by the multiplier. They can be defined as:

$$(M/A) = M/A$$

Where:

(M/A) = overall maximum day multiplier
M = maximum day production
A = average day production

The flows are shown graphically in Figure 1-53 (This discussion will focus on maximum day multipliers although it is also applicable to peak hour, minimum day, minimum hour, or any other multipliers. The multipliers are dimensionless and the flows can be in any consistent flow units.)

The maximum day production and usage can be determined as:

$$M = (M/A) \, A$$

In reality however, both M and A are made up of customer demand and leakage and M and A do not contain the same fraction of each. Average (A) and maximum day (M) use are really made up of:

$$A = AC + L$$

$$M = MC + L$$

Where:

$MC =$ maximum day customer use
$AC =$ average day customer use
$L \ =$ water loss due to leaks

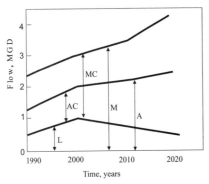

Figure 1-53: Graphical representation of flows

One can reasonably expect MC/AC to remain constant in the future but [MC + L]/[AC + L] is not necessarily constant. Water utility performance in terms of leak detection and repair, or the lack thereof, can change the overall multiplier while MC/AC remains constant. Instead of using overall multipliers, it is generally superior to estimate future maximum day demand using:

$$M = (MC/AC)\ AC_f + L_f$$

Where:

$L_f \ =$ estimate of future year
        leakage
$AC_f =$ estimate of future
        average day metered
        consumption

By treating consumption and leakage independently, it is possible to better account for each in the multipliers. In situations where an overall multiplier is required, the overall multiplier can be given by:

$$(M/A) = [(MC/AC)\ AC_f + L_f]/[AC_f + L_f]$$

In cases where the leakage is small in comparison to consumption, then the above equation can be reduced to:

$$(M/A) = MC/AC$$

However to the extent that leakage is significant, using an overall multiplier can lead to inaccuracy.

Illustrative Example

Consider a system that presently has an average day demand of 5 MGD with 30% leakage (i.e. 3.5 MGD customer demand) and a peak day use of 7.5 MGD. This gives an overall multiplier of 1.50 and a consumption multiplier (MC/AC) of 2.0. If the nature of the customers use does not change (a basic assumption in using any multiplier), then a value of 2.0 should be true in the future while the accuracy of the 1.50 value will depend on how leakage changes over time.

Table 1-2 shows that in a future year, the value of the overall multiplier (M/A) can vary widely but more significantly, the value of the maximum day demand can be significantly in error. In this case, if the utility reduced its percent leakage in half (kept same leakage quantity in spite of increasing system), then the overall multiplier should have increased to 1.85 from 1.5. More significantly however is the fact that even if the average day demands are accurate, the maximum day demand can vary from 15 to 18.5 MGD. This can have a significant impact on utility planning in terms of major facilities such as plants, wells, pipes and pumping stations. The same sort of inaccuracies can occur in any multiplier and individual nodal demands in water distribution system models.

Year	AC	L or L_f	A	%L	M	M/A	MC	MC/AC
Current	3.50	1.50	5.00	30	7.50	1.50	7.00	2.00
Future	7.00	3.00	10.00	30	17.00	1.70	14.00	2.00
Future	5.00	5.00	10.00	50	15.00	1.50	10.00	2.00

Table 1-2: Sample multipliers

Procedure

In order to better estimate future maximum demands, one should first separate current day consumption and leakage (i.e. estimate current day AC, MC and L based on A, M and utility billing records). Then estimate future values of consumption and leakage (i.e. AC_f and L_f). Finally use the formula

$$M = (MC/AC)\, AC_f + L_f$$

to arrive at more accurate future demands. If an overall multiplier is required for some reason, it should be calculated from:

$$(M/A) = [(MC/AC)\, AC_f + L_f] / [AC_f + L_f]$$

Conclusion

The use of multipliers should yield fairly accurate estimates of future peak usage assuming that leakage remains a small portion of the water produced. However, as leakage increases, the use of multipliers may no longer produce reliable results.

Author: Thomas Walski, Ph. D., PE

Genetic Algorithms in Water Resources Engineering

The future of water distribution modeling?

Imagine that you have been assigned the task of designing an expansion for a local municipality's water distribution system. The town's funds for infrastructure improvements have been cut so it is your responsibility to achieve the highest level of operability for each dollar spent. You have worked on similar projects in the past and have developed a sophisticated level of experience using water distribution system computer models. Thus, you are confident that your level of experience applied in conjunction with a simulation model will guide you to an optimal cost-effective solution.

But, would it be possible for computer software to "intuitively" iterate towards the same (or better) solution? This article explores the use of cutting edge genetic algorithms for optimizing water distribution models.

Traditional Modeling Practice

You begin the project by modeling the existing water distribution system using a network modeling software package such as Cybernet® or WaterCAD®. You determine the design criteria, including minimum and maximum allowable pressures and velocities, and then calibrate the model of the existing system to field observed values for a range of operating conditions. Finally, you examine the model for critical deficiencies in the system, such as low pressure or high velocity zones.

Based on projected development, you are able to compute future demands on the system. You add new pipes, pumps, tanks, and valves, and replace or clean any existing ones. Additionally, you adjust any operational settings necessary in order to meet the projected demands on the system. You run the first trial solution, review its performance, and possibly compute the cost. You'll repeat this trial-and-error process until you reach an economically feasible solution that meets the design criteria; hopefully before your deadline is up and your budget has been exhausted.

This is typical of water distribution system modeling projects. Using models such as Cybernet® and WaterCAD®, the experienced modeler can successfully simulate flows, pressures, and tank depletion rates under both existing and future conditions. However, this method of modeling relies on the modeler to identify the trial solutions to be evaluated.

As seen in the above scenario, the modeler depended solely on his or her experience to identify the different trial solutions. While this may be acceptable for very small changes to a water distribution system, even a moderate expansion project can involve billions of possible combinations of pipe, tank, pump, and valve improvements as well as operational settings. Consider a simple network of 20 pipes, where each pipe could be one of ten different diameters. Even if your computer was capable of evaluating one million scenarios in a second, you would need over three million years of computer time in order to evaluate all of the enumerations (Simpson, Dandy, Murphy, 1994). An expansion which considers changes in pumps, valves, or other variables as well, would take considerably longer.

Optimization Techniques

It is unlikely that even the most experienced of water distribution modelers will obtain the optimum solution for even the simple 20 pipe network mentioned above using traditional modeling practices. Although water distribution computer models provide very accurate results, a lot can be done to ensure that they are providing optimum results. Researchers have thus focused their attention on developing methods for automating the optimization of water distribution models.

Early research on the optimization of water distribution models focused on techniques such as enumeration, the evaluation of all possible solutions; and selective enumeration, the evaluation of a selected list of all possible solutions. Enumeration, except when applied to the simplest

"Three billion years of evolution can't be wrong. It's the most powerful algorithm there is." -David Goldberg

of model changes, proved to be a prohibitively expensive and time-consuming technique. Selective enumeration takes less time; however, because the selection process is based on the modelers experience, it does not guarantee that the optimal solution will remain (Simpson et al, 1994).

The most promising method to come out of this research has been the application of genetic algorithms (GAs) to the optimization of water distribution systems. GAs are search algorithms based on the theory of natural selection and the mechanisms of population genetics. They are powerful and adaptive algorithms that have proven to be able to efficiently search complex solution spaces (Simpson et al, 1994).

Genetic Algorithm Optimization

In a 1975 book by John H. Holland of the University of Michigan entitled Adaptation in Natural and Artificial Systems (Holland, 1975), the concept of conducting structured searches for solutions to complex problems using mathematically based artificial evolution or GAs was explored. GAs have since been successfully applied to fields as diverse as the management of investment portfolios, construction scheduling, structural optimization, musical composition, computer chip design, and control systems optimization. For example, U.S. West reported that GA optimization analysis has cut design times for its fiber-optic networks from two months to two days (Begley and McGinn, 1995). It has been in just the last few years that researchers have started to apply GAs to the problem of optimizing water distribution system models.

GA optimization is not a replacement for traditional simulation modeling; instead, it is performed as a next step after simulation modeling. You will still rely on a water distribution system model to layout and calibrate your system. However, instead of relying on the modeler to evaluate different scenarios on a trial-and-error basis, GA optimization automates the solution search process by instructing the computer to successively generate and evaluate possible solutions.

GA optimization is an extremely powerful tool. Starting from an initial set of randomly generated distribution networks, a GA can drive the solution search towards the lowest cost combination of pipes, tanks, pumps, and valves. This is done by generating and evaluating tens or even hundreds of thousands of different combinations. Defending GA optimization, David Goldberg, a GA pioneer, said "Three billion years of evolution can't be wrong. It's the most powerful algorithm there is" (Naik, 1996).

How Do Genetic Algorithms Work?

The GA process generates successive populations of trial solutions, the "fittest" of which survive to breed and evolve increasingly desirable offspring solutions. The trial solutions in a GA are referred to as strings or "chromosomes." They are further composed of a series of characteristics or features (typically coded in binary), analogous to the biological genes found in DNA (Frey, Hransbury, 1997).

In order to begin implementing a GA to solve an optimization problem, the modeler needs to code the decision variables, such as pipe sizes and pump settings, as "genes." For example, different pipe sizes would be assigned unique binary numbers. Consider the following simple scenario. Assume

that you are optimizing pipe sizes for an expansion to an existing water distribution system. You are adding ten pipes to the system, each of which could be one of four unique diameters (Table 1-3).

Pipe Size	Binary Code
6"	00
8"	01
10"	10
12"	11

Table 1-3: Gene coding of pipe sizes

Based on this data, the GA will generate an initial population of say 50 solutions using a random number generator. Each solution will contain a randomly generated pipe size for each of the ten new pipes. The random number generator assigns either a 1 or a 0 to each bit-position in the 20-bit string where each successive two bits represents a specific pipe size for one of the ten pipes (Figure 1-54).

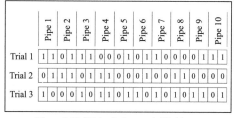

Figure 1-54: Trial solutions coded in binary

Once the initial population is generated, the GA will translate each "gene" into the corresponding pipe size and compute the total cost of materials, construction, and maintenance. A hydraulic analysis will then be performed for each of the solutions in the population and performance deficiencies will be noted. The GA then assigns a penalty cost to each solution (i.e. dollars per unit of headloss) that does not satisfy user-defined criteria such as minimum pressure constraints. A total solution cost is computed from the difference between total cost and penalty cost. The GA will compute a level of "fitness" for each solution in the population based on some function of the total solution cost (Simpson et al, 1994).

The next steps of the process involve the application of the GA operators. In its simplest form, a GA may be comprised of 3 operators:

- Reproduction

- Crossover

- Mutation (Reis et al, 1997)

The following scenario explains one variation of how these operators work. Keep in mind that this explanation covers GAs in their most basic form. There are many variations that can be used to suit whatever optimization problem is at hand.

Reproduction

The probability that a string from the original population of solutions will be selected to reproduce offspring is based on its level of "fitness." The GA selects which solutions are fit to reproduce by using a selection scheme. One such scheme is referred to as the weighted roulette wheel (Goldberg, 1989). The theory is based on a roulette wheel with slots that are sized according to the computed fitness of each solution. Each solution in the population is assigned to the appropriate segment of the wheel; thus, when the wheel is turned, solutions with a higher fitness (i.e. lower total solution cost) will have a higher probability of being selected. The GA simulation will "turn the wheel" once for every solution on the wheel. The solutions that the wheel ends up on will be selected for breeding the next generation of solutions.

Crossover

Next, the crossover operator is applied which initiates a partial exchange of bits between two parent strings to form two offspring strings. The GA will randomly pick 2 solutions for breeding. Based on a user defined probability of cross over, a random number generator will determine if cross over will occur (Simpson et al, 1994). For example, assuming a user defined probability of crossover of 0.80, a random number is generated between 0 and 1.0. If the random number is less than 0.8, the GA will perform cross over. Another random number generator is used to select a crossover point along the solution strings (i.e. position 14 in the 20-bit string). As shown in Figure 1-55, the crossover operator will move the last six digits of the first string in the pair to the last six digit positions of the second string and vice versa.

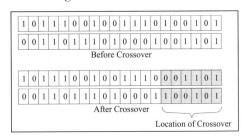

Figure 1-55: Crossover

Mutation

In order to truly emulate the genetic process, a mutation operator needs to be incorporated to account for the random mistakes made by nature. By occasionally flipping values, the mutation operator allows the introduction of new features into the population pool. The GA considers each string in the new generation bit by bit. A random number between 0 and 1 is generated. Assuming a user defined mutation probability of 0.01, the GA will apply mutation only if the random number is less than 0.01. The mutation will consist of changing a 0 to a 1 or vice versa (Figure 1-56).

It is critical that the mutation operator is properly set; too low and you run the risk of losing important genetic material; too high and the search process will degenerate into a random process (Savic and Walters, 1997).

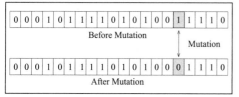

Figure 1-56: Mutation

The steps of the GA process are repeated over and over to generate successive generations of more "fit" solutions until a handful of feasible solutions remain. These solutions can then be evaluated by the decision maker who can further narrow the selection by considering other nonqualifiable measures such as clearance with other underground piping systems.

Applications of GAs

The simple example given above was purely for illustrative purposes and would probably not be a prime candidate for a GA. Below are a few possible water distribution problems which would benefit significantly from GA optimization.

- Pump scheduling for large or complex distribution systems.

- Setting operational points for water tanks, pumps, and pressure valves.

- Blending of water sources to meet water quality standards at minimum costs.

- Locating and sizing system storage to meet equalization, fire flow, and emergency needs most efficiently (FWE, 1996).

- Optimize the location of control valves in a water supply network in order to maximize leakage reduction (Reis et al, 1997).

GAs in Practice

As you would expect, the most important reason to undertake a GA optimization of a water distribution system would be to save money. As an example, a water district in Colorado used GA optimization in 1997 to reevaluate its 2015 master plan prepared by traditional modeling practices. They found that a $5.85 million improvement plan could be built for approximately $3 million using an optimized design. Further review determining which portions of the optimization were feasible resulted in a 20% savings (Roe, 1998).

The major drawback of current GA optimization for distribution systems is that run times for larger networks (several thousand pipes), may require 10-15 hours for a complete analysis, making it extremely expensive. Although proponents of the technology claim that you'll get the money back in construction savings, the technology will need to improve before it becomes widely accepted as a viable optimization option. Current research at places such as the University of Exeter (United Kingdom), the University of Illinois, and the University of Colorado will hopefully advance the technology so that it can tackle the more involved optimization problems in a cost effective manner.

Author: Adam M. Strafaci

References

American Water Works Association (AWWA). 1992. "Distribution System Requirements for Fire Protection," AWWA Manual M31, Second Edition, Denver.

Begley, S., McGinn, D. 1995. Software au Naturel. *Newsweek* (May 8): 70-1.

Cesario, A.L., Kroon, J.R., Grayman, W.M., and Wright, G. 1996. New Perspectives on Calibration of Treated Water Distribution System Models., Proc. AWWA Annual Conference, Toronto, Canada.

Clark, R.M., Grayman, W.M., Goodrich, J.A., Deininger, A.F., and Hess, A.F. 1991. Field-Testing Distribution System Water Quality Models. *Journal AWWA*, vol. 83, No. 7.

FWE, Inc. 1996. GA Optimization Applications & Benefits. URL: http://www.frey-water.com/benefits.htm.

Frey, J., and Hransbury, J. 1997. Saving Money Through the use of Optimization Analysis. *Water/Engineering & Management* 144 (August): 30-2.

Goldberg, D.E. 1989. *Genetic Algorithms in Search, Optimization and Machine Learning.* Reading, MA: Addison-Wesley Publishing Company.

Grayman, W.M., Clark, R.M. Males, R.M. 1988. "Modeling Distribution-System Water Quality: Dynamic Approach", J.WRPMD, ASCE, Vol. 114, No. 3.

Haestad Press. 1997. *Practical Guide to Hydraulics and Hydrology.* Waterbury, CT: Haestad Press.

Herrin, G. 1997a. Calibrating the Model. *Practical Guide to Hydraulics and Hydrology.* Waterbury, CT: Haestad Press.

Herrin, G. 1997b. An Example Calibration of a Water Distribution System Model. *Practical Guide Hydraulics and Hydrology.* Waterbury, CT: Haestad Press.

Holland, J. H. 1975. *Adaptation in Natural and Artificial Systems.* Bradford Books.

Naik, G. 1996. Back to Darwin: In Sunlight and Cells, Science Seeks Answers to High-Tech Puzzles. *Wall Street Journal* (January 16): A1-3

Reis, L. F. R., Porto, R. M., and Chaudhry, F. H. 1997. Optimal Location of Control Valves in Pipe Networks by Genetic algorithm. *Journal of Water Resources Planning and Management* 123 (November/December): 317-26.

Roe, A. 1998. Water Distribution Engineers Apply Darwin's Theory to System Design. *ENR* (August 3) 104-5.

Rossman, L.A. 1997. When Has a Model Been Sufficiently Calibrated and Tested to be Put to Efficient Use. Forum in J.EE, ASCE, Vol. 123, No. 11.

Rossman, L.A., Clark, R.M., and Grayman, W.M. 1994. Modeling Chlorine Residuals in Drinking-Water Distribution Systems. L.EE, ASCE, Vol. 120, No. 4.

Savic, D. A., and Walters, G. A. 1997. Genetic Algorithms for Least-Cost Design of Water Distribution Networks. *Journal of Water Resources Planning and Management* 123 (March/April); 67-77.

Simpson, A. R., Dandy, G. C., and Murphy, L. J. 1994. Genetic Algorithms Compared to Other Techniques for Pipe Optimization. *Journal of Water Resources Planning and Management* 120 (July/August): 423-443.

Vasconcelos, J.J., Boulos, P.F., Grayman, W.M., Kiene, L., Wable, O., Biswas, P., Bhari, A., Rossman, L.A., Clark, R.M., and Goodrich, J.A. 1996. Characterization and Modeling of Chlorine Decay in Distribution Systems. AWWA Research Foundation, Denver, company

Walski, T.M. 1995. Standards for Model Calibration, AWWA Computer Conference, Norfolk, VA.

Walski, T.M. 1984. Analysis of Water Distribution Systems, Kreiger Publ. Melbourne, FL.

Geographic Information Systems

Geographic Information Systems: an Introduction to the Technology

Develop an understanding of GIS and what
it can do for your projects.

Almost everyone working in the civil engineering field utilizes maps in some form or another. They may be topographic maps for site development, road maps for infrastructure, or water distribution maps for city planning. Whatever the project, maps are a source of valuable information that engineers need for their design process.

Large projects often require that vast amounts of data be extracted from maps. Databases are thus useful as an efficient and effective means of storing, organizing, and retrieving the data. Simply put, a Geographic Information System (GIS) is a link between maps and databases.

For those in the civil engineering field who are not utilizing GIS, this article is for you. Without getting into overwhelming detail, this article will provide a brief introduction to the technology and the buzz words that go along with it. Additionally, it will answer questions such as what a GIS can do for you and your projects, what are the components of a GIS, and how does a GIS work? Although by no means is this article meant to be a substitute for the hundreds of books on GIS, it will hopefully spark interest and encourage the development of more civil engineering GIS applications.

What is a GIS and What Does it Do?

There is really no universally accepted definition for a GIS. One GIS manufacturer defines it as a computer-based tool for mapping and analyzing things that happen on earth by integrating common database operations such as query and statistical analysis with the visualization and geographic analysis benefits of maps (ESRI, 1998). The Federal Interagency Coordinating Committee (FICCDC, 1988) defines GIS as "a system of computer hardware, software, and procedures designed to support the capture, management, manipulation, analysis, modullary, and display of spatially referenced data for solving complex planning and management problems." (Antenucci et al, 1991). Other definitions emphasize that the key feature of a GIS is the analysis of data to produce new information. Whatever definition you prefer, it is generally accepted that a GIS will perform the following key tasks:

• Import data

• Manage data

- Query and Analyze data

- Visualize data

Import Data

Probably the most time intensive step in setting up a GIS is getting all of your data sets into the GIS in a consistent format and at a consistent scale. Although you may be manually entering some of your data into a database, more frequently you will be extracting data from preexisting sources. Most GIS systems support the use of digitizing and scanning for converting paper maps into digital files. Existing digital files, such as AutoCAD® drawings, can also be imported. Additionally, there are numerous tools available for manipulating the data once it is in the GIS to ensure consistency in format. For example, as discussed later in this article, there are tools to convert data between different coordinate and projection systems.

Manage Data

As mentioned earlier, GIS is essentially a map linked to a database. Thus, a basic understanding of how databases organize information is useful before working with GIS. GIS manages the underlying data in a Database Management System (DBMS). Typically, the relational database model is used which stores data in a collection of tables that are linked together by common fields (Figure 2-1).

Query and Analyze Data

Once you have input data and your GIS is functioning, you can begin to tap its power by performing queries. For example, you can perform simple queries such as what percentage of area is developed as single family homes or what is the distance between two places. More useful,

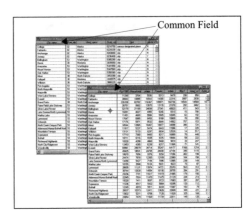

Figure 2-1: Tables in a relational DBMS

however, are the powerful analytical capabilities of a GIS. You can perform a proximity analysis to determine how many factories are within a 20 mile radius of a pollution sampling site. You can also perform an overlay analysis that integrates at least two data layers to answer complex questions. For example, you can overlay land use, soil type, and subbasin maps to determine curve numbers for a hydrologic study.

Visualize Data

A GIS is used to perform queries and analysis so that you are able to make informed decisions. Whether you are using it to link billing records to your water distribution model or for determining the impact of urban sprawl on the spotted owl population, it is essentially a high powered decision support tool. This brings us to the last capability of a GIS, visualization. The results of a GIS query combined with the visualization capabilities can help to create high impact documents which are easy to interpret. GIS allows you to integrate maps with reports, graphs, photographs, and more to turn your results into powerful tools for the decision makers (Figure 2-2).

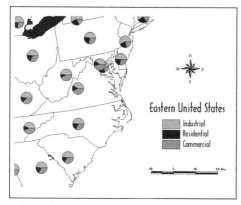

Figure 2-2: Data visualization using ESRI's ArcView

Components of a GIS?

Hardware

A GIS is composed of hardware, software, data, and methods or rules. Unlike the infancy of GIS which required the use of mainframes, today's applications can now be run on a wide range of hardware types including desktop PC's, servers, and high powered graphics workstations. This has led to a dramatic increase in the user base and has resulted in a huge market for GIS software and applications.

Software

A range of GIS software is available to provide the necessary functions for storing your data, analyzing your data, and visualizing it. Some of the major players in the GIS software industry are ESRI, Autodesk®, and MapInfo. It is important to note that approximately 80% of all GIS applications are customized for the organization that is using it (Wilson, 1998). Thus, most of the popular GIS packages are built around an open ended architecture which allows the user to customize the application often with proprietary programming languages. Accordingly, beyond the developers of the actual GIS engine, there are hundreds of companies out there that will develop custom applications for your use.

Data

The most critical element of any GIS is of course the data itself. Data can be collected in house, purchased from a data provider, or obtained via the Internet. Internet sites for U.S. Government agencies such as the U.S. Geological Survey (USGS) are a great place to start looking for data. The following are some of the more common data types you will encounter :

- Digital Elevation Model (DEM) – A DEM is a set of digital topographic data developed by the USGS. DEMs, which are recorded in a raster format (defined in the next section), typically follow the 7.5-minute quadrangles of the USGS topographic series.

- Triangular Irregular Network (TIN) – A TIN is an organization of spatial information based on a set of irregularly shaped triangles that form a connected network. TINs are used to efficiently organize surface data with minimal redundancy.

- Digital Line Graph (DLG) – DLGs, also known as 100K DLGs, are developed by the USGS. The data are vector based (defined in the next section) in the form of digitized lines at a scale of 1:100,000. DLGs are available for several categories of data including contours, roads, and rivers. (Chou, 1997)

- Topologically Integrated Geographic Encoding and Referencing (TIGER)/Line® files – TIGER® is the name for the system and digital database developed by the U.S. Census Bureau to support its mapping needs for the Decennial

Census and other U.S. Census Bureau programs. TIGER/Line® files are a digital database of geographic features, such as roads, railroads, rivers, lakes, political boundaries, census statistical boundaries, etc. for the entire United States. The database contains attributes of these features such as their location in latitude and longitude, the name, the type of feature, address ranges for most streets, the geographic relationship to other features, and other related information (U.S. Census Bureau, 1998).

Methods

The final component of a GIS is a bit more abstract. Building a GIS is a complex and resource intensive process, thus it is important that the developer establish an objective and plan before collecting any data. The objective should incorporate business specific rules or methodologies. Without a well defined direction, the effectiveness of the GIS will most likely be lost in a clutter of unorganized data. By establishing a sound objective early in the project, the developers can focus on the areas of the GIS that will provide the most benefits at the least cost, thereby maximizing the utility of the system.

How Does GIS Work?

Understanding how GIS works requires an in depth understanding of the following subjects.

- Relating information from different sources

- Data capture

- Data integration

- Projection and registration

- Data structures

Because of the introductory nature of this article, the following are brief descriptions of these key concepts. Before delving into the construction of a GIS, additional reading on these subjects is essential.

Relating Information From Different Sources

The power of a GIS comes from its ability to relate information from disparate sources. A GIS can be used for converting existing digital information, which may not be in map format, into forms it can recognize and use. For example, digital satellite images can be analyzed to produce a thematic layer of digital information about vegetation. Additionally, existing tabular data such as census or hydrologic information can be converted to map-like format.

In order for data to be usable in a GIS it needs to be referenced to the map in some way. This is achieved through explicit and implicit geographic references. An explicit reference defines a specific location on the earth's surface through a line of latitude or longitude or a national grid coordinate. An implicit reference, on the other hand, is a description such as an address, postal code, census tract name, or road name. Through an automated process known as geocoding, explicit references can be created from implicit references.

Data Capture

The process of getting data into a digital format recognized by the GIS is known as data capture. Data on existing paper maps can be digitized or hand-traced using a mouse in order to collect the coordinates of features. Electronic scanning devices are another alternative. Data capture is typically the most time consuming step in creating a GIS and whether you are digitizing or manually entering data in tabular format, you can expect to spend a lot of time editing or removing extraneous data.

Data Integration

A GIS stores information as a collection of thematic layers which are linked together by geography (Figure 2-3). Underlying these layers are associated tables of spatial and descriptive attributes that describe the geographic features (Figure 2-4). A GIS allows you to link and integrate layers of existing information that would be difficult or too time intensive to associate through other means.

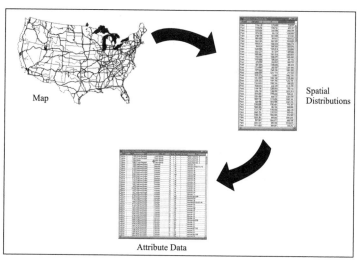

Map

Spatial Distributions

Attribute Data

Figure 2-4: Tables of spatial and descriptive attributes

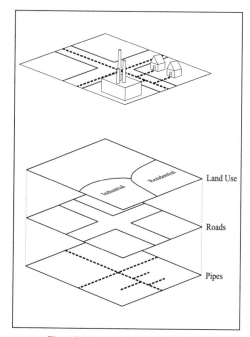

Land Use

Roads

Pipes

Figure 2-3: Integration of thematic layers

Projection and Registration

When obtaining information from different sources it is critical that it is all converted to a consistent spatial reference before it is used in the GIS. This is done through a process called registration which aligns all of the data layers. Establishing a consistent coordinate system for your data layers will aid in the registration process. Most GIS systems will convert data between coordinate systems as well as allow the user to define their own coordinate system.

In addition, before data can be analyzed it may need to go through a process called projection. Projection, one of the fundamental components of mapmaking, is the mathematical method of transferring information from the Earth's three-dimensional surface to a two-dimensional medium. There are many map projections available, however, each of them will result in distortion of one or more of these properties: shape, area, distance, and direction. Depending on the project, and the ultimate purpose of the maps, the optimal projection system will vary.

Map projections are a science in themselves, thus an in-depth discussion would be inappropriate for this article. To introduce the concept, the following is a look at the most widely adopted map projection in GIS applications, Universal Transverse Mercator (UTM).

UTM divides the surface of the Earth into 60 equally divided zones, each covering a width of 6 degrees in longitude (See Figure 2-5). This is done to eliminate the distortion that occurs as you increase the distance from a specific line of longitude (or meridian). UTM projection is thus useful only for relatively narrow zones (i.e. 6 degrees longitude).

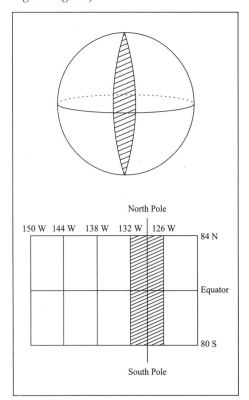

Figure 2-5: Universal Transverse Mercator projection (Chou, 1997)

As you proceed north and south of the equator on the surface of the earth, the distance between the meridians bounding a UTM zone decreases. You can visualize this by looking at the surface of a globe. In order to transform the surface of the earth to a flat surface, the UTM projection system assumes that between 84 degrees north latitude and 80 degrees south latitude, there is a negligible change in distance between the bounding meridians. As a result, UTM zones can be represented as rectangular areas (Figure 2-5) (Chou, 1997).

Data Structures – Raster vs. Vector

Graphic images can be stored as either raster or vector. The raster method organizes spatial features in a regularly spaced grid of cells or pixels. The vector data structure, on the other hand, organizes spatial features by a set of vectors which are specified by starting point coordinates, a direction, and a length. Figure 2-6 shows a land use map organized in both the raster and vector data structures.

The smallest point feature in a raster data structure is represented by a single pixel and has an implied area equivalent to the size of the pixel. The following are some of the advantages of the raster data structure.

- Map overlays can be efficiently processed if thematic layers are coded in a simple raster structure.

- Because the raster grid defines units or pixels that are consistent in size and shape, spatial relationships among pixels are constant and easily traceable.

- The raster model typically provides a better representation of continuous surfaces.

- A large amount of available spatial data such as satellite imagery and scanned aerial photographs are already in a raster structure.

Some of the disadvantages of the raster format are:

- If you have a large area with the same feature, i.e. land use, a simple raster structure would result in a huge number of pixels of identical value. This will result in data redundancy.

- Linear features such as rivers, pipes, and roads are poorly represented with a raster data structure.

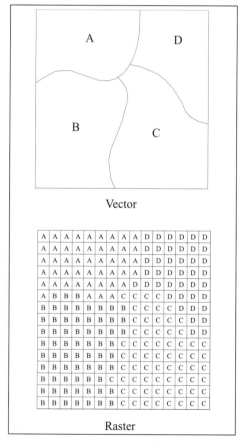

Figure 2-6: Vector vs. Raster data structure

- Data transformation of raster data typically results in distortion. For example, if a pipe represented in raster format is rotated and then rotated back to its original position, it may be different from its original shape.

- The computation and processing accuracy of spatial features represented in a raster data structure is usually less than desired. For example, computing the length of a pipe in raster structure is not as simple as computing the length between the two bounding nodes. (Chou, 1997).

Vector data structures can be used for point, line, and polygon features. Point features are represented as vectors with no length or direction. Lines are designated by a sequence of vectors and polygons are represented by a series of vectors that form an enclosed area. Contrary to a line designated in raster format, a vector line is one-dimensional and has no width associated with it. Some of the advantages of the vector data structure are the following.

- The vector data structure provides a way of organizing large quantities of information with minimal data duplication. For example, a large field can be defined by its bounding polygon instead of as thousands of pixels all with the same data associated with them.

- Features such as roads or pipes can be represented clearly and continuously.

- The vector data structure supports greater precision in the computation and processing of spatial features. For example, the length along a river is easily computed as the cumulative length of the lines that form it.

The most significant disadvantage of the vector data structure is that computations involving map overlay are not nearly as straight forward as they are with the raster model. For example, while determining if a specific point is located within a certain area is simple with a raster model, it becomes an involved task with a vector model. A methodology known as "point-in-a-polygon," is used to solve such problems. The type of GIS software used will govern how "point-in-a-polygon" is implemented (Chou, 1997).

Conclusion

The intent of this article was to answer some basic questions about GIS and to spark your interest in its far reaching potential. As previously mentioned, hundreds of books have been written on GIS, ranging from introductory texts to theoretical journals. Thus, if you consider implementing a GIS, vast resources are available for guidance. In the mean time, with the introdutory material provided in this article you should have the knowledge to start brainstorming potential applications for integrating your data and maps to efficiently solve your problems.

Author: Adam M. Strafaci

Distributed GIS: The Future of Geographic Information Systems

Interoperability standards and distribution of geographic information over the Internet will revolutionize the use of GIS.

" I believe we need a 'Digital Earth.' A multi-resolution, three-dimensional representation of the planet, into which we can embed vast quantities of geo-referenced data…Like the web, the Digital Earth would organically evolve over time, as technology improves and the information available expands." This is the vision presented in Vice President Al Gore's January 31, 1998, speech "The Digital Earth: Understanding our planet in the 21st Century" (Gore, 1998). The speech, which was given at the California Science Center in Los Angeles, served as an open invitation for the private and public sector to join in applying spatial information technology to a wide range of challenges and problems.

The concept of the Digital Earth may appear to many as something out of a science fiction movie; however, as technologies such as GPS, satellite imaging, and GIS rapidly converge on the Internet, such a vision is becoming a real possibility. In fact, most of the technologies and capabilities required to build such a system are either available now or are currently under development. Whether you are involved in a global project, such as the Digital Earth, or a local one, such as a county master plan, you will at some time be obtaining and distributing geographic information over the Internet.

This article introduces you to interoperability standards, one of the major pitfalls associated with obtaining geographic information over the Internet, and what is being done to eliminate it. Additionally, a conceptual framework of distributing geographic information over the Internet is presented.

Interoperability

One of the many strengths of a GIS is its ability to integrate many disparate data themes to find solutions to complex problems. A valuable source for obtaining such data themes is via the Internet. Unfortunately, as those who have tried will attest to, downloading geographic information is often a cumbersome and time-consuming method for obtaining and distributing data. The user needs to first navigate the Internet to find the appropriate data and then download the data in its entirety. Because each GIS platform has its own proprietary system for storing data, the user must then convert the data to a format understood by their software. Finally, the user can integrate the data with the other themes that they are using. If GIS software were able to read GIS data in a consistent manner, regardless of the brand of the data server or the GIS client, or where they were located on a local or global network, client users, data consumers, data providers, and software vendors would benefit greatly.

Let us first consider the growth of the Internet. The Internet has succeeded to become the massive force that it is because of the emergence of a few simple, widely agreed upon protocols such as the Hypertext Transfer Protocol (HTTP) and the File Transfer Protocol (FTP). Likewise, in order for GIS to grow and for concepts such as the Digital Earth to materialize, some level of interoperability must be developed so that geographical information generated by one software package can be read by another. Fortunately, the GIS industry is already well on its way towards addressing interoperability issues through groups such as the Open GIS Consortium (OGC) and the Interoperability Advisory Group (IAG). The following is an overview of the roles these two organizations are playing in the development of universal GIS standards.

OGC

The OGC is a non-profit organization made up of GIS vendors, developers, and other parties with a stake in the GIS industry whose mission is to develop software interface standards that enable seamless communication between different geoprocessing systems. The OGC envisages a distributed computing environment which includes GIS clients scattered across an Intranet or the Internet that can communicate with one another and access shared data. Unlike exchange formats such as the familiar DXF format generated by AutoCAD, OGC's interoperability standards involve software tiers on the clients and servers of future GIS products. Ultimately, a desktop GIS package fitted with an interface conforming to OGC will be able to access data and services from a GIS data server with its own OGC interface (McKee, 1998a).

The initial OGC specification, referred to as the OGC Simple Features Implementation Specifications, describes the mechanics of how different GIS systems will "speak" to one another about geometry (points, lines, polygons), spatial reference systems, and geographic attributes (McKee, 1998a). Specifically, the specifications cover the following computer industry interoperability standards :

- Object Linking and Embedding/Component Object Model (OLE/COM),

- Common Object Request Broker Architecture (CORBA), and

- Structured Query Language (SQL).

Future OGC Specifications will include OGC Coverages and Catalogs. Products which are submitted to OGC for review may conform to one, some, or all of the specifications. Products that pass the tests will receive a trademark license from OGC which specifies how the product can use the OGC certification mark (McKee, 1998b). The certification mark on products will indicate that the product will interoperate with other products carrying the same mark.

As with the development of Internet standards, the goal of GIS interoperability is an international endeavor. The OGC has and will continue to extend its influence globally by working with organizations such the International Standards Organization (ISO) TC/211, the technical committee tasked by ISO to prepare a family of geographic information standards (OGC, 1998a); Japan's National Spatial Data Infrastructure Promoting Association; Europe's Joint Research Center; and key universities. Relationships such as these will continue to lay the foundation for global initiatives such as the United Nations' Global Spatial Data Infrastructure.

IAG

The IAG was established in 1996 to support and promote the work of the OGC within the federal government and to provide an open forum for IAG members to stay informed about government geospatial issues (OGC, 1998b). The IAG is made up of over 60 members including GIS companies, integrators, and other information technology companies with interests in geoprocessing whose main goals are to:

- address federal spatial data policy,

- help draft legislation, and

- hold public meetings (McKee, 1998c).

The Internet and the Future of GIS

There are several model architectures for the way we will obtain geographic information in the future. One such model is a network-oriented distributed GIS where the user will be able to obtain GIS functionality over the Internet using the World Wide Web. This architecture, which has been proposed by Environmental Systems Research Incorporated (ESRI), is based on the integration of four technologies (ESRI, 1997):

- Client/Server computing,

- Object-oriented design,

- Java, and

- GIS.

Client/Server Computing

Most of us are familiar with the concept of the client/server model where information and applications are stored on one or more servers, which can be accessed by any number of computers (clients) connected by a network. Typically, the model works in a question-and-answer fashion where the user on the client end enters requests or commands which are then sent to the server. The server then uses its stored information (applications and data) to answer the request by returning information to the client (Figure 2-7).

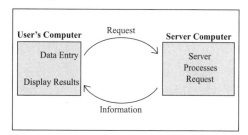

Figure 2-7: Standard client/server architecture

Similarly, a network-oriented GIS user will be able to send messages from a local machine (client) to a remote GIS engine (server) to invoke a specific GIS function or a collection of functions. While the server is static, the client will change dynamically based on the user's requests and actions. To reduce Internet traffic, network-oriented GIS establishes a new client/server architecture that is slightly different from traditional client/server applications. Instead of a constant connection, the connection between client and server is active only when the client communicates with the server. Figure 2-8 shows a schematic of the workflow within a network-oriented distributed GIS.

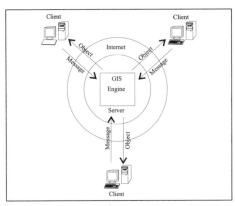

Figure 2-8: Client server architecture for network-oriented distributed GIS (ESRI, 1997)

tied to a specific central processing unit and thus can be run on any computer with the appropriate interpreter known as a Java Virtual Machine. This platform independence is clearly an advantage for usage in a distributed GIS system where performance across multiplatform networks will be imperative. A further advantage is in how Java deals with the vector formats on which most GISs operate. Currently, HTTP can not support vector data formats making it difficult to directly display vector data on the Internet. Java applets can manipulate and display vector data on the assigned browser display area.

Object-Oriented Design

Eighty percent of GIS applications are customized for use at each organization (Wilson, 1998). Thus, there is a great need to simplify the customization process. By utilizing object-oriented design, developers will be able to create robust GIS applications that can be reused, refined, tested, maintained, and extended, thus increasing their return on investment. Using the concept of abstraction, object-oriented design will enable the decomposition of the GIS system into objects, which are the basic components of the design. By creating each component so that they will be able to operate independently, the client will be able to request specific GIS components over the Internet from the GIS server in order to construct a customized application to meet their needs.

Java

Java, developed by Sun Microsystems, has rapidly become a household term. Java is an object-oriented programming language primarily used for developing web based applications called applets. The power of Java, and the cause of all the hype surrounding it, is its platform independence. Because Java is an interpreted language, it is not

Conclusion

The integration of already existing technologies, or the development of new technologies, will most definitely make some sort of distributed GIS system possible in the near future. As the ease with which geographic data is distributed over the Internet increases, and as interoperability becomes standard, engineers will be able to access and utilize data to solve complex problems. The ability to easily share data will increase productivity, decrease project durations, and reduce costs.

Author: Adam M. Strafaci

References

Antenucci, J. C., Brown, K., Croswell, P. L., Kevany, M. J., and Archer, H. 1991. *Geographic Information Systems a Guide to the Technology*. New York: Van Nostrand Reinhold.

Chou, Y-H. 1997. *Exploring Spatial Analysis in Geographic Information Systems*. Santa Fe, New Mexico: OnWord Press.

ESRI. 1997. The Future of GIS on the Internet: An ESRI Whitepaper (June).

ESRI. 1998. About GIS (July7). URL: http://www.esri.com/library/gis/abtgis/what_gis.html.

FICCDC Technology Working Group. A process for evaluating Geographic Information Systems. *Technical Report 1*. U.S. Geological Survey Open-File Report 88-105 (1200).

Gore, A. 1998. "The Digital Earth: Understanding Our Planet in the 21st Century." California Science Center, Loas Angeles, CA. (January 31). URL: http://www.opengis.org/info/newsletter/9804/digearth.htm.

Haestad Press. 1997. *Practical Guide to Hydraulics and Hydrology*. Waterbury, CT: Haestad Press.

McKee, L. 1998a. Open GIS Connection: OGC Supports Gore's Digital Earth. *GIS World* (June).

McKee, L. 1998b. What Does Open GIS Specification Conformance Mean? *GIS World* (August).

McKee, L. 1998c. Waking Up Washington. *GIS World* (October).

Open GIS Consortium, Inc. (OGC). 1998a. OGC and ISO TC/211 News. URL: http://www.opengis.org/info/newsletter/9804/iso_tc_211.htm.

Open GIS Consortium, Inc. (OGC). 1998b. IAG News. URL: http://www.opengis.org/info/newsletter/9804/iag_news.htm

Plewe, Brandon. 1997. *GIS Online: Information, Retrieval, Mapping, and the Internet*. Santa Fe, New Mexico: OnWord Press.

U.S. Census Bureau. 1998. TIGER® Overview (March 25). URL: http://www.census.gov/geo/www/tiger/overview.html.

Wilson, J.D. 1998. Java Expected to Energize GIS. *GIS World* (August).

Special Topics In Stormwater and Floodplain Modeling

Step-by-Step Inlet Design with the New FHWA Standards

Understanding the principles of inlet design.

Road and highway design must include sufficient provisions for drainage to minimize the danger resulting from storm runoff and to optimize travel efficiency under most weather conditions. Thus, the practicing engineer must understand the principles governing inlet and gutter design. The following provides a review of the concepts underlying inlet and gutter design.

The key objective in inlet design is to minimize the spread of water across a roadway. The allowable spread length, generally determined by local or state regulations, is based on the classification of the road. For example, if the road being constructed has a higher speed limit, the spread should be minimized to a greater degree than slower speed roads because of the increased risk of hydroplaning. In addition to spread width, roadway classification also dictates the return period of the design storm an engineer should use to test the viability of their drainage design. Table 3-1 provides a comprehensive overview of different road conditions and the design criteria these conditions necessitate.

Other good sources for inlet and drainage information besides your state Department of Transportation (DOT), are the Federal Highway Administration's (FHWA) HEC-22 manual (Brown et al, 1996) which now replaces HEC-12, and the American Association of State Highway and

Road Classification		Design Return Period	Design Spread
High Volume or Divided or Bi-Directional	<70 km/hr (45 mph)	10-year	Shoulder + 1m (3ft)
	>70 km/hr (45 mph)	10-year	Shoulder
	Sag point	50-year	Shoulder + 1m (3ft)
Collector	Low Volume	10-year	½ Driving Lane
	High Volume	10-year	Shoulder
	Sag Point	10-year	½ Driving Lane
Local Streets	Low Volume	5-year	½ Driving Lane
	High Volume	10-year	½ Driving Lane
	Sag Point	10-year	½ Driving Lane

Table 3-1: Various road classifications and design criteria(Brown, Stein, & Warner, 1996)

Transportation Officials (AASHTO, 1991) drainage manuals. These manuals detail every aspect of the inlet design process from the appropriate equations to in-depth descriptions of the most common inlet classes.

Gutter Sections on Grade

Gutter sections are defined by the variables depicted in Figure 3-1. HEC-22 makes a distinction between uniform gutter sections ($S_w = S_x$), and composite gutter sections ($S_w > S_x$). The variation in slope between S_w and S_x results in a gutter depression, indicated as *a*, measured at the face of the curb.

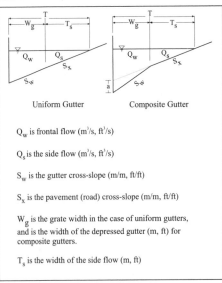

Uniform Gutter   Composite Gutter

Q_w is frontal flow (m³/s, ft³/s)

Q_s is the side flow (m³/s, ft³/s)

S_w is the gutter cross-slope (m/m, ft/ft)

S_x is the pavement (road) cross-slope (m/m, ft/ft)

W_g is the grate width in the case of uniform gutters, and is the width of the depressed gutter (m, ft) for composite gutters.

T_s is the width of the side flow (m, ft)

Figure 3-1 : Uniform and composite gutter sections

On a road with a constant grade, spread should be at its maximum at the location of the inlet. Note that the spread at this location is totally independent of the inlet efficiency. The spread is only a function of the geometry and roughness of the road and gutter sections. At a given inlet, the spread is not controlled by the inlet, it is controlled by the spacing and efficiency of the upstream inlets. Therefore, if spread is too large, the inlets need to be spaced closer with each inlet being allocated smaller catchment areas to maintain a correct level

of gutter discharge, or the upstream inlets need to be more efficient.

Runoff in gutters on grade is considered to be open channel flow, so Manning's equation is applicable. The Manning equation is integrated for an increment of width across the section resulting in:

$$Q = (K_c/n)\, S_x^{1.67}\, S_L^{0.5}\, T^{2.67}$$

Where:

Q = flow rate (ft³/sec, m³/s)
K_c = 0.56 (0.376 in SI units)
n = Manning's coefficient
S_x = cross slope (ft/ft, m/m)
S_L = longitudinal pavement slope
T = width of flow or spread (ft, m)

Solving this equation is simple for uniform gutters where the spread T, can be explicitly calculated for a given flow rate Q. However, in the case of composite gutters where Q is expressed as a function of T, it becomes much more complicated to solve for T. Since T can no longer be expressed as an explicit function of Q, the use of software such as FlowMaster® 6.0 and StormCAD® 3.0, both of which will calculate the spread by an iterative process, will prove time saving.

Problem Statement: *All examples in this article are based on the following conditions. Consider a road which supports a high traffic volume through a suburban commercial center. The road has a speed limit of 45 mph, is situated on a grade of 1%, and has 3 m lanes with 1.5 m shoulders on both sides. The road has a 4% gutter cross slope, and a 2% road cross slope. The rainfall from a 10-yr storm causes a runoff of 0.045 m³/s on the catchment for the road inlet.*

Example 1: *Using the information in the above problem statement, FlowMaster® 6.0 is used to compute the initial spread in the gutter (Figure 3-2). The spread of 1.64 m was calculated using Manning's equation for a composite gutter.*

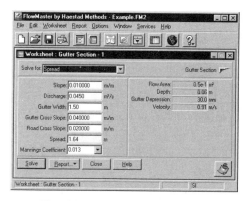

Figure 3-2 : Summary of spread calculations

Inlets on Grade

The three major types of inlets are grate, curb opening, and combination (grate and curb opening). For these inlets, the greater the longitudinal slope and the greater the flow, the greater the tendency for the flow to physically skip or pass over the inlet and not be intercepted. The flow that is not captured is referred to as bypass or carryover flow.

Inlet design equations solve for the efficiency of the inlet:

$$E = Q_i / Q$$

Where:

E = inlet efficiency (dimensionless)

Q_i = flow intercepted by inlet (ft³/s, m³/s)

Q = total discharge in gutter (ft³/s, m³/s)

Grate Inlets

An engineer needs to choose an appropriate grate inlet for the roadway being designed. Bicycle traffic, for example, would limit choices to those with longitudinal and transverse bars to maintain appropriate safety standards. Each configuration of bars has different splash over velocities, which are the velocities that occur when runoff achieves

enough momentum to splash over the top of the grate without being intercepted. Typical splash-over velocities, which are functions of the grate type and the grate length, can be obtained from the grate manufacturer or the HEC-22 manual published by the FHWA (Brown et al, 1996).

Another characteristic associated with different grate types is their propensity for clogging. For example, a grate with longitudinal bars clogs less readily than a grate with crosshatches or reticuline patterns (Figure 3-3). For a more comprehensive list of grate types refer to the HEC-22 manual (Brown et al, 1996).

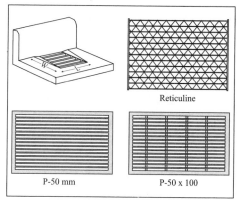

Figure 3-3: Various grate configurations

Equations associated with grates calculate the ratio of the intercepted frontal flow to the total flow, R_f, and the ratio of the intercepted side flow to the total side flow, R_s.

Therefore, the total intercepted flow is:

$$Q_i = R_s Q_s + R_f Q_f$$

Where:

R_s = ratio of intercepted side flow to total side flow

R_f = ratio of intercepted frontal flow to total frontal flow

---

Essential Hydraulics and Hydrology

Example 2: *Consider a P-50 mm type grate with a length of 1 m and a width of 0.6 m. Utilizing FlowMaster® to solve for efficiency results in a grate efficiency of 82% (Figure 3-4). Notice that the frontal flow factor for the gutter and grate system is 1.00 while the side flow factor is 0.22. In order to maximize this grate efficiency, you need to maximize the frontal flow. This can be achieved by increasing the gutter cross slope.*

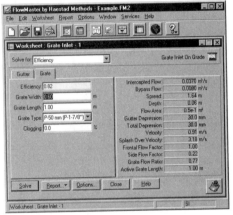

Figure 3-4: Summary of interception calculations

Curb Inlets

Curb inlets are openings within the curb itself and are used in areas where grate inlets are prone to clogging (Figure 3-5). The efficiency of the curb

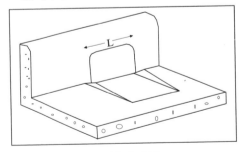

Figure 3-5 : Curb inlet

inlet is based on the ratio of the inlet length (L) to the length necessary to capture 100% of the total runoff. Curb inlets are often inset into the asphalt several inches to create a local depression. Note that the local depression, *a'* (Figure 3-6) is entirely different from the gutter depression, *a*, that results from the variation between the gutter and road cross-slopes.

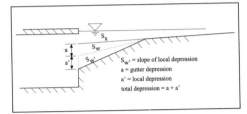

Figure 3-6 : Local depression

The efficiency of the curb inlet is:

$$E = 1 - (1 - L/L_T)^{1.8}$$

Where:

E = curb inlet efficiency

L = length of the curb inlet (ft, m)

L_T = length of the curb inlet required to capture 100% of the flow (ft, m)

Again the intercepted flow is calculated by multiplying the efficiency, E, times the total flow, Q.

Example 3: *Consider a curb inlet with a length of 1.2 m. Using FlowMaster® to solve for efficiency results in a curb inlet efficiency of 38% (Figure 3-7), nearly half of the overall capacity of the grate inlet in the previous example. Typically, the only recourse an engineer has to positively affect the efficiency of the inlet, short of altering the road itself, is by increasing the length of the curb opening.*

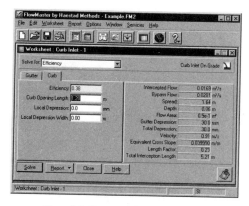

Figure 3-7 : Summary of curb calculations

Combination Inlets

As you may suspect, combination inlets are inlets with both grate and curb openings (Figure 3-8).

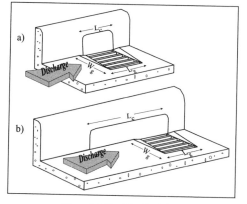

Figure 3-8: Combination inlets

The curb inlet functions as a sweep, removing debris from the flow to prevent the grate from clogging. If the curb inlet length (L_c) is equal to the grate inlet length (L_g) then the flow intercepted is approximated by the flows that would be intercepted by the grate inlet alone (Figure 3-8a). The curb inlet may be extended out in front of the grate to act as a sweeper. This configuration serves to remove approaching debris before it has an opportunity to become clogged in the grate

(Figure 3-8b). The total flow intercepted by a sweeper inlet is calculated as the sum of:

- the flow intercepted by the portion of the curb opening located upstream of the grate,

- the remaining flow (flow that passed the upstream curb opening portion) intercepted by the grate.

Example 4: *Consider a combined inlet with a 1.2 m curb inlet with no local depression combined with the same grate inlet used in the previous example. The combined inlet is similar to the second configuration shown in Figure 3-8b. Solving for efficiency results in a combined inlet efficiency of 83% (Figure 3-9), only a meager improvement over the grate alone. The same factors that will increase the efficiency for the grate and the curb inlets will increase the efficiency for the combined inlet. Thus, for economic reasons, the combined inlet is only necessary if grates in the area have a propensity to clog.*

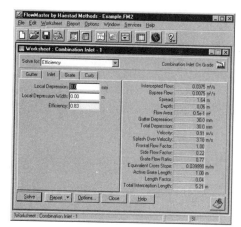

Figure 3-9: Summary of combination inlet calculations

Inlets in Sags

Inlets located in sag are assumed to collect 100% of the flow to avoid severe ponding. As opposed to inlets located on a grade, the efficiency of inlets in sag directly affects the spread. HEC-22 (Brown et al, 1996) recommends employing at least a 50-year design storm when calculating the capacity of an inlet located in a sag.

The intercepted flow computations for inlets in sag are based on the principles of weir flow and orifice flow.

The capacity of an inlet without a local depression or gutter depression operating as a weir is:

$$Q_{iw} = C_w P d^{1.5}$$

Where:

Q_{iw} = flow intercepted by the inlet ($ft^3/s, m^3/s$)

C_w = weir coefficient which varies depending on the flow condition and inlet structure

P = perimeter of the inlet (ft, m)

d = flow depth at curb (ft, m)

Note: For a grate inlet the perimeter does not include the length along the curb. For a curb inlet the perimeter is equivalent to the length of the inlet.

If the inlet is submerged and is operating as an orifice, its capacity becomes:

$$Q_{io} = C_o A (2gd_o)^{0.5}$$

Where:

Q_{io} = flow intercepted by the inlet as an orifice ($ft^3/s, m^3/s$)

C_o = orifice coefficient which varies based on the class of inlet and its configuration

A = area of the inlet opening (ft^2, m^2)

g = 32.16 ft^2/s (9.80 m/s^2 in SI units)

d_o = effective head at the center of the orifice throat (ft, m)

A common practice is to take the minimum intercept value (Q_{iw}, Q_{io}) calculated from the orifice and weir equations and use that as the most conservative design point for calculating the inlet efficiency.

Grates alone are not typically recommended for installation in sags because of their propensity to clog up and exacerbate the ponding during severe weather. Curb inlets have various geometries depending on the configuration of the inlet throat. The three most common throat geometries are horizontal, vertical and inclined (Figure 3-10). In the case of orifice flow, the flow depth, d_o, used to calculate the intercepted flow is specific to each of the different throat types, so be aware of the differences.

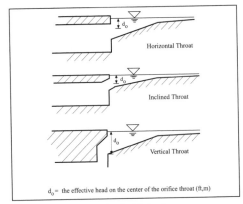

d_o = the effective head on the center of the orifice throat (ft,m)

Figure 3-10 : Curb inlet throats

At low flow depths, a combination inlet in sag, acting as a weir, operates much the same way as a grate inlet alone. At higher flow depths both the curb and grate act as orifices working in conjunction. The total intercepted flow is then calculated as the sum of the flows intercepted by the grate and the curb opening, both acting as orifices.

Conclusion

A combination inlet is expected to have a greater efficiency than the grate or the curb opening alone. But simply using a combination inlet may not be the most expedient solution. If grate inlets in the area are not prone to clogging, then an alternative solution may be to extend the length of the grate in order to achieve comparable results. Or if the road is still in design phase a steeper gutter cross-slope would in turn increase the gutter frontal flow (on grade situation) or the water depth at the curb (in sag situation) resulting in more efficient inlets.

Although, the calculations for inlet design are important, it is necessary to have a comprehensive understanding of the location and the surrounding conditions in order to create the most efficient and cost effective design. These conditions include the road classification, the design speed, traffic volumes, and whether the inlet is located on a grade or in a sag.

With the knowledge of the surrounding area and local regulations, the engineer can determine the design storms and acceptable spread to design an adequate inlet and gutter system. The design process is greatly simplified when computer software, such as Haestad Methods' FlowMaster® 6.0 or StormCAD® 3.0, is used to perform the calculations quickly and to display the results conveniently.

Author: Benjamin White

Redefining Rainfall Classification with the Haestad Severity Index

Understand and overcome the limitations of rainfall event definitions.

Phrases such as "*5-year rainfall*" or "*100-year storm*" are commonly used in everyday life to describe rainfall events. However, these phrases are generally confusing to the general public and insufficient for practicing engineers. For an average news listener, a phrase such as "*5-year event*" does not say much about the severity of the rainfall event. In addition, this phrase is not of much help to a practicing engineer since it does not include the duration of the rainfall event in question. This paper suggests a new method of classifying rainfall events. The proposed Haestad Severity Index (HSI) categorizes rainfall using ten levels of magnitude.

Are Return Periods Alone Adequate?

The idea of a *return period* is generally confusing to non-engineers and its loose definition can be easily misused or misunderstood by engineers. A rainfall event is said to have a return period of *T-years* if a rainfall with larger magnitude occurs on average every *T* years. For decades, engineers and meteorologists have been using return periods to describe the severity of rainfall events. However, using return period alone does not really provide sufficient description since the return period does not define the rainfall's duration.

It is often theorized that designing with the 2-year through 100-year return events provide enough "variety" to ensure that detention ponds will operate properly under a wide range of potential rainfall conditions. This paper explains why this approach may not always provide the expected "wide" range of rainfall conditions.

This article proposes a new concept that uses HSI levels (1 through 10) to define the magnitude of "real world" and synthetic design rainfall events. This new approach allows engineers to easily report to the general public the relative magnitude of any rainfall event, regardless of rainfall duration and total rainfall depth.

Confusing the Public

The return period of a rainfall event is defined as the inverse of the event's exceedance probability. For example, if there is a 10% probability (P) that a certain event will occur within any given year, the return period (T) is calculated as $T = 1/P = 10$-year event. To the general public, this definition might imply that a rainfall event of this magnitude will occur about every ten years. But because this definition is based on probability, it is possible that a 10-year event could occur more than once within that 10-year period, and possibly even within a given year. Therefore, the definition of a return period sends mixed signals to the general public.

Misleading Orders of Magnitude

For multistage detention design, the typical design rainfalls are the 2, 5, 10, 25, 50, and 100-year events. At first glance, it appears that the 2-year event is a very small event compared to the 100-year event. Some engineers may even wrongly deduce that the 2-year event looks as though it should be about 2% of a 100 year event.

Table 3-2 shows the relative rainfall depths with respect to the 100-year event for Northwestern Illinois in the United States. Note that the 2-year 24-hour rainfall depth is approximately 40% of the 100-year event. Or in other words, the 2-year event is almost one half the size of the 100-year event!

Return Period (years)	24-hour Depth (in)	Depth Relative to 100-yr
2	3.11	42%
5	3.95	59%
10	4.63	63%
25	5.60	76%
50	6.53	89%
100	7.36	100%

Table 3-2: Total and relative 24-hour rainfall depth for Northwestern Illinois (Huff and Angel, 1989)

The previous example compares different rainfall events of the same duration, namely 24-hour rainfall events. Even more confusion is introduced when we compare rainfall events of different durations. From Table 3-3 we can see that the

Return Period (years)	1-hour Depth (in)	24-hour Depth (in)
2	1.46	3.11
5	1.86	3.95
10	2.18	4.63
25	2.63	5.60
50	3.07	6.53
100	3.51	7.36

Table 3-3: 1-hour and 24-hour Rainfall Depth for Northwestern Illinois(Huff et al, 1989)

2-year 24-hour event has a larger rainfall depth (3.11 in) than the 50-year 1-hour event (3.07 in). Does this mean that the 2-year event is more severe than the 50-year event? Not necessarily. Severity of a rainfall event is defined by both its return period and its duration. We can not talk about a rainfall magnitude if we do not define both the event's return period and event's duration.

Gaping Holes for "Small" Events

The 2-year 24-hour event is typically used as the smallest detention design storm in many parts of the United States. This criteria means that the smallest event analyzed is typically about one half the magnitude of the 100-year event. This design approach ignores small events (crucial to good water quality design), resulting in structures that may potentially flush small events downstream with little or no attenuation or detention time. For example, a 1-month rainfall event may be sufficient to flush off parking lot pollutants such as automobile oils and heavy metals that build up over time. This highly polluted runoff flows straight through detention structures with little to no impedance, unless the outlet has been designed to attenuate very small rainfall events. Therefore, better criteria is also needed for events significantly smaller than the standard 2-year 24-hour event.

Return Period vs. Flooding Potential

The current classification of a rainfall event's relative magnitude is typically based on return period. This definition, however, does not necessarily correspond to the potential flood damage. For example, Figure 3-11 shows a 100-year ½ hour depth of 2.86 in., compared to a 100-year 24-hour depth of 7.7 in. Although both events are technically defined as the 100-year event, does each event really have the same flood impact on the watershed? Furthermore, how could the general public distinguish between these two 100-year events? These questions are difficult to answer using the currently accepted storm classification system.

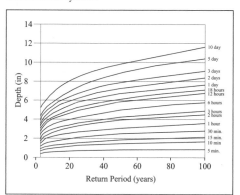

Figure 3-11: Rainfall Depth/Duration/Frequency Curves for Northwestern Illinois (Huff et al, 1989)

Currently, a rainfall event is typically described using return period only. While the return period gives us some information about the relative "magnitude" of the event, the actual flood damage potential also depends on rainfall duration and watershed characteristics. Incorporating both rainfall return period and rainfall duration could potentially achieve a more realistic representation of relative magnitude for a given rainfall event.

Case Study: Misleading Public Message

Suppose a local newspaper publishes an article discussing minor flood damage that had resulted from an early summer thunderstorm. The rainfall event was approximately one hour in duration with about four inches of total rainfall depth. This event washed out a few rural culvert crossings and caused other minor damage. The newspaper correctly reports that the event was classified as a 100-year event.

Suppose the article then went on to compare the event to a flood of record that occurred decades earlier which was also (properly) classified as a 100-year event. Technically the article would be correct by definition, but misleading. The flood of record was based on a 100-year total rainfall depth of 10 inches for a rainfall duration of about 10 days, inundating large urbanized areas with flood depths of up to several feet over city streets! Even though the rainfall events had dramatically different total rainfall volumes, they could both be technically described as a "100-year event" for this geographical region.

Wanted: New Storm Classifications

Previous sections have identified some of the problems with current rainfall classifications. A new rainfall classification system is needed to define how a particular event compares in severity with other rainfall events. Well designed categories provide relative comparison from one level to the next, and can be easily understood by the general public. Hurricanes and tornadoes are designated using levels of severity, and earthquakes are described using the Richter scale. Rainfall return periods provide an amorphous classification that lacks a true correspondence to potential danger. Conversely, if a weatherman could report the approach of a level 7 storm, the public could more easily associate the appropriate level of caution.

In addition, it is important for the classification to be based on the entire range of engineering necessity. A level 1 rainfall event can not be so meager as to have no practical design application. For example, as mentioned above, the minimum level 1 event should be something on the order of a 1-month, 15-minute event that is capable of flushing significant pollutants from a parking lot. Alternatively, a level 10 event should correspond to events commonly recognized as a maximum design rainfall event. On FEMA Flood Insurance Rate Maps, the 500-year event is the largest event mapped. The 10-day duration rainfall event is typically the maximum duration available in localized rainfall tables. Therefore a 500-year, 10-day duration rainfall event could potentially serve as an ideal level 10 storm under a new classification system.

Defining the Haestad Severity Index

By classifying severity levels as a function of duration and probability (return event), we can construct a dimensionless severity index that could theoretically be applied anywhere in the world. Natural streams and channels evolve over thousands of years as a direct result of the localized rainfall conditions. Therefore, a level 8 event could theoretically pose the same flood potential for two different regions of the world, even though their total rainfall depths are significantly different for the given return period and duration (assuming the watersheds are subjected to similar antecedent conditions and urbanization levels).

For urbanized areas, facilities are designed to accommodate a certain range of events based on local statistical rainfall for various return events. Therefore, a level 6 event would theoretically pose the same flood potential for two different urbanized geographical regions, even though their total rainfall depths are different for the given return period and duration.

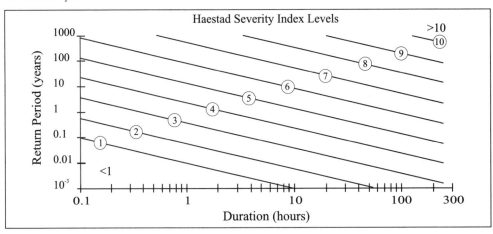

Figure 3-12: Haestad Severity Index Levels

This paper proposes a new subjective classification system for defining rainfall severity. Figure 3-12, which demonstrates severity levels 1 through 10, was constructed based on the assumptions and mathematical relationships outlined below.

In defining the levels, two assumptions were made. First, the severity of a rainfall event is directly proportional to the duration of the event. Secondly, the severity of a rainfall event is directly proportional to the return period of the event. With these two assumptions, a relationship was developed to relate the severity to duration and return period.

$$S_L = DR$$

Where:

S_L = severity index level
D = duration (hours)
R = return period (years)

Two boundary conditions were selected to encapsulate the scope of practical engineering necessity. Level 1 represents the smallest rainfall magnitude that might be useful to engineers for analyzing parameters such as pollutant loadings in water quality analyses. The boundary point for Level 1 was selected as a 0.1-hour, 0.1-year rainfall. Level 10 represents an event that is potentially of "catastrophic" magnitude. The boundary point for Level 10 was selected as the 10-day (240 hour), 500-year event since floodplain studies are rarely analyzed for rainfall events larger than this magnitude.

The severity index for the level 1 and level 10 storms are computed as:

$$S_1 = 0.1 * 0.1 = 0.01$$

$$S_{10} = 240 * 500 = 120,000$$

Each duration will have a corresponding return period for that severity index, and if R vs D is graphed on a log-log plot the relationship forms a straight line.

The other severity indexes were calculated by dividing the difference between the natural logs of S_1 and S_{10} by 9 to yield the spacing, K, between the remaining 8 levels.

$$K = [\ln(S_{10}) - \ln(S_1)] / 9$$

$$K = [\ln(120,000) - \ln(0.01)] / 9$$

$$K = 1.81116$$

The new severity index, S_L, for each corresponding severity level, L, then becomes:

$$\ln(S_L) = \ln(S_1) + K*(L-1).$$

Example 1: *Constructing severity level 5*

The following demonstrates how points are constructed along a line for severity index level 5.

$$ln(S_5) = ln(.01) + 1.81116 \times (5-1)$$

$$ln(S_5) = 2.6395$$

$$S_5 = 14.006$$

The return event can then be solved for any duration using the relationship:

$$S = DR$$

Solving for return event, this can be rearranged as:

$$R = S/D$$
$$= 14.006 / D \text{ (for Level 5 event)}$$

Solving this equation for return event given standard durations yields the results presented in Table 3-4. The same procedure is used for the other severity levels.

Duration (hours)	Return Period (years)	Severity Level 5 Index
0.1	140	14.006
0.25	56	14.006
0.5	28	14.006
1	14	14.006
2	7	14.006
3	4.7	14.006
6	2.3	14.006
12	1.2	14.006
18	0.78	14.006
24	0.58	14.006
72	0.19	14.006
240	0.06	14.006

Table 3-4: Duration/Return period data for a Level 5 event

Example 2: *Case Study Revisited*

How would the previous newspaper case study classify the given rainfall events using severity levels? As shown in Figure 3-13, the 100-year 1-hour event would be approximately a level 6 event. The 100-year 10-day event would be greater than a level 9 event. This new rainfall classification system would therefore demonstrate a relative difference between these two events, even though they are both technically "100 year events".

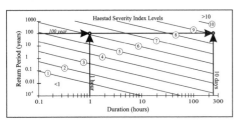

Figure 3-13: Example 2

Example 3: *Using the Severity Index*

Suppose a thunderstorm rolled through the geographical area corresponding to the rainfall data in Figure 3-11. If the storm deposited approximately 2.8" in about 2 hours, what is the return frequency and severity level?

Step 1) Using Figure 3-11, determine that a duration of 2 hours and a depth of 2.8" correlates to a 10 year return period.

Step 2) Using Figure 3-14, determine that a return period of 10 years and a duration of 2 hours will yield a severity level of about 5.

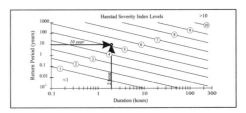

Figure 3-14: Example 3

Snowmelt Adjustments

Some of the worst floods on record resulted from a combination of heavy rain and snowmelt. In these situations three phenomena increase the severity of the event: 1) the melting snow adds a significant volume of water; 2) the snow has increased the antecedent moisture of the soil; and 3) areas of heavy ice and snow allow little or no infiltration into the soil.

The HSI level of a given rainfall event can account for snowmelt using the following procedure:

$$P_a = (P_r + P_{sm}) \times R_{sm}$$

Where:

P_a = adjusted total rainfall depth applied to given duration

P_r = total rainfall depth for given duration

P_{sm} = rainfall equivalent depth based on snow depths

R_{sm} = estimated increased runoff potential based on snow & ice conditions

Note: Application of this formula requires the selection or derivation of methods for estimating P_{sm} and R_{sm}.

Example 4: *Adjusting for Snowmelt*

Suppose a late winter rainfall event deposited 4" of rainfall over 48 hours within a mountainous region. This rainfall depth and duration combination represents about a 5 year return event for the given geographical area. Local authorities project that an unusually large depth of existing snow cover in the area will add an additional 3" of snowmelt water to the event. Due to increased antecedent moisture conditions and impervious ice surfaces, the authorities estimate an increased runoff potential (over normal conditions) of about 1.4.

What is the HSI level based on rainfall only, and the HSI level adjusted for snowmelt and runoff potential?

From Figure 3-12, read an HSI level of about 6.5 (for rainfall only) for a 48 hour duration, 5 year event.

$P_a = (4"\ rainfall + 3"\ snowmelt) \times 1.5 = 10.5"$

For this particular geographical area, the adjusted rainfall depth of 10.5 inches correlates to about a 500 year event for a 48 hour duration event.

From Figure 3-12, read an HSI level of about 9.0 for a 48 hour duration, 500 year event.

In this example the HSI level was raised from 6.5 to 9.0 when accounting for snowmelt conditions.

Antecedent Moisture Adjustments

The HSI levels proposed in this article are based on "normal" antecedent moisture conditions for the given geographical region. If successive rainfall events have significantly raised the moisture content of the soil, then infiltration will be reduced, increasing the runoff compared to normal conditions.

The HSI level of a given rainfall event can account for wet antecedent soil moisture conditions using the following procedure:

$$P_a = P_r \times R_{am}$$

Where:

P_a = adjusted total rainfall depth applied to a given duration

P_r = total rainfall depth for a given duration

R_{am} = estimated increased runoff potential based antecedent soil moisture conditions

Note: Application of this formula requires the selection or derivation of methods for estimating R_{am}.

Example 5: *Adjusting for wet soil conditions*

Suppose a late spring event deposited 2.8" of rainfall over 6 hours. This rainfall depth and duration combination represents about a 5 year return event for the given geographical area. This area has received extremely high depths of rainfall within the last few days resulting in near saturated soil conditions. The local authorities estimate that these soil conditions will result in an increased runoff potential of about 2.0.

What is the HSI level based on rainfall only, and HSI level adjusted for snowmelt and runoff potential?

From Figure 3-12, read an HSI level of about 5.0 (for rainfall only) for a 6 hour duration, 5 year event.

$$P_a = (2.8" \text{ rainfall}) \times 2.0 = 5.6"$$

For this particular geographical area, the adjusted rainfall depth of 5.6 inches correlates to about a 10 year event for a 6 hour duration.

From Figure 3-12, read an HSI level of about 7.0 for a 6 hour duration, 100 year event.

In this example the HSI level was raised from 5.0 to 7.0 when accounting for adverse moisture conditions.

Proposed New Design Storms

The 2, 5, 10, 25, 50, and 100 year (24- hour) events are typical detention design storms in the United States. This criteria has two major deficiencies: the smallest storm depth is almost one half the size of the largest storm, and all storms are for the same (relatively long) duration.

The concept of severity levels classifies rainfall "magnitude" using a much more versatile set of rainfall relationships that include both duration and return period. The proposed design storms shown in Figure 3-15 begin with a short duration and small return period, which could be useful for water quality analyses. Both the duration and return period are gradually increased to establish a design storm that falls approximately within each of severity levels one through eight. This approach could potentially reflect varying degrees of total rainfall depths and durations, resulting in detention designs that handle a variety of rainfall conditions – from very small water quality events to the maximum spillway design event.

Design points were established using standard durations and return events. Table 3-5 displays a proposed set of rainfall events for detention pond design using Figure 3-11 to obtain the depths. Note how the proposed events demonstrate a much more comprehensive range of design depths compared to events typically used (see Table 3-2).

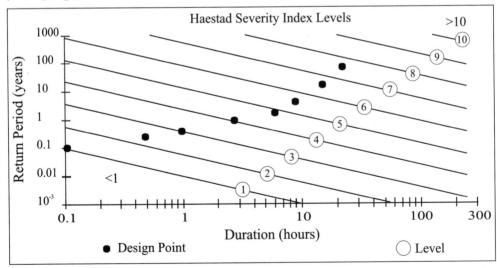

Figure 3-15: Proposed Design Storms

Severity Index Level	Return Period (years)	Duration (hours)	Example	
			Depth (inches)	Depth Relative to 100-year
1.0	0.1	0.1	0.1	1%
2.8	0.5	0.5	0.78	10%
3.5	1	1	1.22	16%
4.5	2	3	2.01	26%
5.4	5	6	3.02	39%
6.2	10	12	4.07	53%
6.9	25	18	5.18	67%
7.8	100	24	7.7	100%

Table 3-5: Developing design storms using severity index levels

HSI Strengths

The proposed Haestad Severity Index has many advantages:

- leverages current existing data

- considers duration as well as return period

- applies to any geographic area

- provides an easy way to estimate rainfall severity

- considers more variables useful to performing risk analyses

- accounts for snowmelt via custom adjustments

- accounts for antecedent soil moisture via custom adjustments

- establishes an easy-to-understand "measuring stick" for the general public

HSI Limitations

The proposed severity index may best serve as simply the first iteration towards defining a new standard for classifying rainfall events. Other variables such as watershed size or different slope(s) for the severity lines could be considered to further differentiate the level of severity between various types of rainfall events. Furthermore, this classification system only refers to the amount of rainfall and does not account for levels of runoff or actual flood impacts.

Subjective return periods and durations were chosen for defining the level 1 and level 10 rainfall event. Levels 2 through 9 were then constructed in equally spaced increments. Future research or more elaborate statistical methods could potentially result in different upper and lower boundaries and/or varying spacing between sequential levels.

The slope of the lines that define the different severity levels were constructed using a simple equation that is based on a subjective relationship between return period and duration. Future research, or perhaps more elaborate statistical techniques could be used to modify the slope of severity level lines to better represent the true severity potential of each depth and duration combination.

For a given rainfall event, the total rainfall volume increases with watershed size. For example, a 6 inch rainfall event will have a much more significant impact if it falls over 50 square miles, versus a localized rainfall event of 6 inches that only falls over a few hundred acres. Future versions of the severity level concept could perhaps incorporate watershed area. Different severity index graphs similar to the ones in this article could be developed for various watershed size categories (such as 0-1 square miles, 1-5 square miles, etc.)

Severity index levels refer to the "magnitude" of a rainfall event as a function of return period and duration. In urbanized areas with poor drainage facilities, a "level 3" rainfall event could theoretically cause more localized damage than a "level 6" event in the same geographical region for an urbanized area with excellent drainage facilities. Therefore this approach is limited to describing the amount of water that reaches the ground, not necessarily the flood impacts generated from the resulting runoff.

Conclusions

Return periods are typically the current method used to define the severity of rainfall events. This definition is confusing to the general public, and does not adequately account for the effects of storm duration. Therefore, very different rainfall events with varying total rainfall depths could fall under the definition of a "100 year event", even though the resulting total rainfall volume could differ dramatically.

Any classification system is subjective to some degree. The proposed severity classification system in this article attempts to categorize rainfall events in a logical fashion. The concept of rainfall severity index levels (1 through 10) attempts to represent a wide range of rainfall events, while providing a description that is easily visualized by the general public.

Coauthors: Michael K. Glazner, Benjamin White, Sasa Tomic, Ph.D.

Pond Routing Techniques: Standard vs. Interconnected

When are interconnected pond modeling techniques required instead of standard pond routing methods?

This article explains the difference between standard pond routing and interconnected pond routing techniques. Through the use of examples, it demonstrates how these two approaches differ and why. The conclusion includes tips on determining which pond routing techniques may apply to your next project.

Pond Routing Overview

Detention ponds are typically used to attenuate and control increased stormwater runoff due to development. Pond routing is a mathematical procedure that models a detention pond's response to a given storm event. By routing a stormwater hydrograph through a pond, engineers can determine how the water surface elevation, outflow and storage values vary during (and after) the storm.

The computed results may vary depending on which mathematical routing technique is used, so it

is important for engineers to readily identify which routing techniques apply to the given conditions.

History

Pond routing techniques were originally established as a means to hand-compute the operation of large reservoirs (lakes) and spillways. Although repetitious, these hand methods were a practical way of assessing the response of large facilities before the advent of computers.

We apply these same techniques when analyzing detention ponds. The difference is that detention models use a much smaller scale in terms of volume, inflow and outflow, and sometimes in terms of time step.

The Working Relationship

Various names have been used to describe "standard" pond routing techniques. Routing methods such as Storage Indication, Modified Puls and Level Pool Routing are all based on the same fundamental relationship:

$$\Delta V = \Delta t \,[\text{Avg. Inflow} - \text{Avg. Outflow}]$$

Where:

ΔV = change in pond volume during one time step (ft^3, m^3)

Δt = time step length (hours)

For each time step on the inflow hydrograph, this equation is solved to compute the change in storage for that single time step. If the average inflow is greater than the outflow, change in storage is positive and the water surface is rising. If the average inflow is less than the outflow, change in storage is negative, and the water surface is receding.

Standard Pond Routing

The Basic Concept

Figure 3-16 demonstrates the fundamental assumption used in standard pond routing. Notice that the downstream pond does not affect the hydraulics of the upstream pond. In addition, the downstream pond is unaffected by the free outfall conditions. Standard pond routing techniques could be used to analyze both ponds shown in this figure.

The Key to Standard Routing: Tailwater (TW) is Fixed or Flow Dependent

Standard routing techniques apply if the tailwater is fixed or if the downstream water surface is a function of flow rate only (not time or downstream volume).

Examples of Fixed TW or Flow Variant TW Elevation:

• Free outfall

• Fixed (constant) outfall elevation

• Outlet outfall water surface elevation based on downstream channel normal depth (solved using equations such as Manning's)

• Outlet outfall water surface elevation solved using backwater rating table of downstream elevation vs. flow (from programs such as HEC-2 or HEC-RAS).

When these assumptions apply, the total outflow for all elevations in the pond can be modeled with a single performance curve like the one shown in Figure 3-17. During the routing process, outflow can be solved as a direct function of pond headwater depth using this curve.

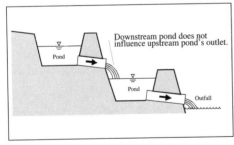

Figure 3-16: Standard pond routing

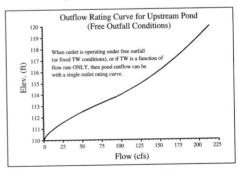

Figure 3-17: Outlet performance curve

Software That Performs Standard Routing

Since standard routing techniques are repetitive, they are ideal for computers. Mainframe programs such as the Army Corps of Engineers' HEC-1 and the Soil Conservation Services' TR-20 were used for reservoir routing more than 25 years ago.

In the mid-1980s, these programs were ported to run on PCs, and private sector software such as the Pond Pack (released in 1987) was written specifically for use in detention pond design. Each of these programs can model standard reservoir routing techniques.

Example 1: Standard Pond Routing

This example demonstrates a case where standard pond routing techniques apply. The results from this example will be compared with Example 2 for an interconnected pond scenario.

Given: The two ponds in Figure 3-18 are directly connected with a box culvert. The downstream pond discharges through a box culvert with a free outfall into the receiving river.

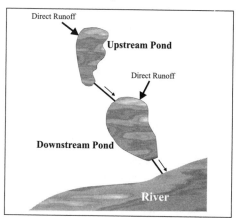

Figure 3-18: Standard pond routing example

The Analyses:

The runoff hydrographs draining into each pond are shown in Figure 3-19. Standard routing techniques were performed to model the pond elevation, storage and outflow during an entire storm event.

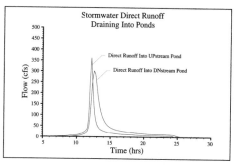

Figure 3-19: Drainage runoff to ponds

Standard routing results for this scenario will be appropriate only if the maximum water surface elevation of the downstream pond does not rise high enough to affect the discharge rate of the upstream pond.

Figure 3-20 shows the water surface elevations in both ponds during the course of the storm. The maximum elevation in the downstream pond stays below the upstream pond's outlet, so standard routing results are valid.

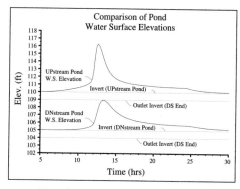

Figure 3-20: Elevations for standard routing

Figure 3-21 and Figure 3-22 display the inflow and outflow hydrographs for the upstream and downstream ponds. These routing results are applicable since the outfall water surface does not affect the downstream pond and the downstream pond water surface does not affect the upstream pond.

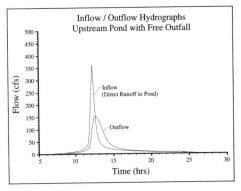

Figure 3-21: Upstream pond results

Conclusions for Example 1:

Figure 3-20 demonstrates that the downstream pond's maximum water surface stays below the outfall invert of the upstream pond's outlet invert. So for the given storm, the downstream pond does not affect the outflow rate of the upstream pond, thus verifying the assumption of standard routing conditions and results shown in Figure 3-21 and Figure 3-22.

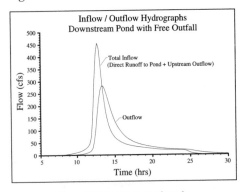

Figure 3-22: Upstream pond results

Therefore, standard routing techniques are applicable to this scenario (with free outfall to the river).

Interconnected Pond Routing

The Basic Concept

Figure 3-23 shows the fundamental relationship involved with interconnected pond routing. Notice how the downstream pond rises to a level high enough to influence the hydraulics of the upstream pond's outlet.

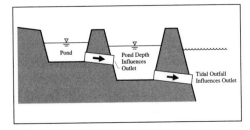

Figure 3-23: Interconnected ponds

Tidal outfall conditions (water surface elevation that varies with time) may also require interconnected routing analyses. Figure 3-23 shows a tidal outfall that rises high enough to influence the downstream pond's outlet hydraulics.

The Key to Interconnected Analyses: Time Variant Tailwater Conditions

When two or more ponds are directly connected and have inverts at or near the same elevations, the water surface elevation in the downstream pond(s) might affect the outflow rate from the upstream pond. This situation produces time variant tailwater conditions since the water surface in each pond is a function of inflow, outflow, pond shape, pond size and pond outlet structures – all operating over time.

*Examples of Time Variant
Tailwater Elevation:*

- Two (or more) ponds connected, with little or no vertical relief between pond inverts

- Tidal outfall into the ocean

- Outfall into time variant stream stage elevations

New Algorithms

In time variant tailwater situations, standard routing techniques will no longer apply if the downstream water surface elevation rises high enough to affect the outflow from the upstream pond. Interconnected pond routing techniques involve complex convergent algorithms that take into account the changing water surface elevation in each pond over the course of time.

The basic mass balance for pond routing still applies to interconnected pond routing, with one major exception: time variant tailwater conditions. For each time step, the outflow is a function of the water surface elevation in the downstream pond, which is a function of the volume, inflow and outflow of that pond .

For standard routing techniques, tailwater is assumed to be a function of flow rate only and can be solved directly based on the water surface in the pond. This technique can not be applied to interconnected analyses since the tailwater is not simply a direct function of flow.

Software for Interconnected Pond Routing

The new version of Pond Pack handles time variant tailwater conditions for interconnected ponds and tidal outfalls. It handles reverse flow and can simulate flap gates (restricts flow to one direction).

This new software can model multiple interconnected pond outfalls (diversions) in a single watershed. It also models conditions where multiple ponds discharge into a single common pond, as well as conditions where a single pond discharges (diverts) into multiple downstream ponds.

Example 2: Interconnected Ponds

This example demonstrates a case where interconnected pond routing techniques apply. Results from this example will be compared with Example 1 for standard pond routing.

Given: Figure 3-24 models the identical pond system and storm event described in Example 1. The only exception is time variant tailwater at the river outfall.   Figure 3-25 shows the flood stage information used for the outfall in this example.

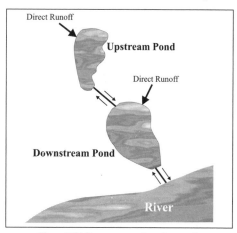

Figure 3-24: Interconnected pond example

If the river elevation rises high enough, it can impact the performance of the downstream pond, which, in turn, could impact the performance of the upstream pond. If the river rises high enough, it can potentially cause reverse flow conditions into the ponds (since there are no flap gates on the outlets).

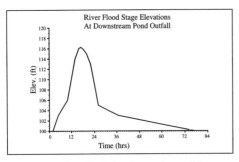

Figure 3-25: Flood elevations at river outfall

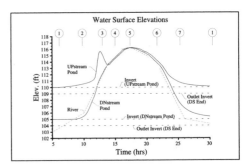

Figure 3-26: Routing results: elevations

The Analyses:

The runoff hydrographs into the ponds are the same ones used in Example 1 (see Figure 3-19). Interconnected routing techniques were performed to model pond elevations, storage and outflow during the storm.

Figure 3-26 displays the computed water surface elevations for each pond, based on interconnected routing. Seven different relationships are designated with circled numbers. These circled numbers also correspond to Figure 3-27.

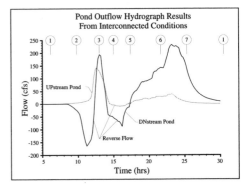

Figure 3-27: Routing results: hydrographs

The schematic profiles on the next page (Figure 3-28) demonstrate conditions for the seven cases circled in Figure 3-26 and Figure 3-27.

Special Note:

Interconnected conditions do not require a tidal outfall as shown in these examples.

Two ponds will have interconnected effects as long as the water surface elevation in one pond affects the outflow of the other pond.

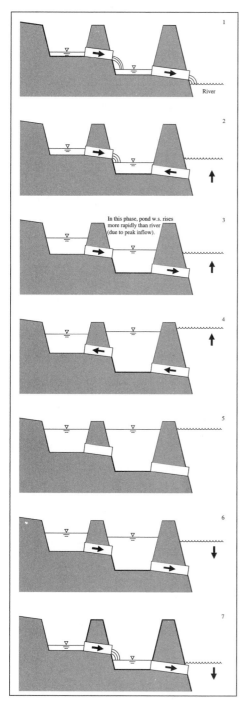

Figure 3-28: Schematic profiles

Conclusions for Example 2:

We see from Figure 3-26 and Figure 3-27 that interconnected pond routing was necessary since the river flood stage rose high enough to affect the downstream pond. In turn, the water surface elevation in the downstream pond rose high enough to affect the discharge of the upstream pond. Standard routing techniques are not applicable for this situation.

The schematic profiles shown on this page demonstrate how several different flow conditions (including reverse flow) can occur within a single routing event. Interconnected routing techniques can simulate each of these cases and when they occur.

On the rising leg of the river flood stage (profile case 2), reverse flow into the downstream pond is occurring, causing the downstream pond elevation to rise and "keep pace" with the rising river. Then between hours 12 and 14 (profile case 3), the downstream pond switches to forward flow because the combined flow from the upstream pond outlet and the direct runoff "outpaces" the rise in the river flood stage.

Comparing Results

This comparison between two examples will demonstrate the potential differences between standard routing and interconnected routing techniques. Example 1 modeled a free outfall scenario using standard routing techniques, whereas Example 2 modeled a flood stage table at the outfall point.

By comparing the water surface elevations and outflow hydrographs from these two examples, we can show how the downstream water surface assumptions can dramatically impact the routing results. In this comparison, standard routing results would be inappropriate for the scenario in Example 2, where a high flood stage coincides with the pond outflow.

Comparison for Upstream Pond

Figure 3-29 compares water surface elevations in the upstream pond. Notice the dramatic difference between the two examples. The backwater effects from the river flood stage prolonged the time that the water remained at a high level in the pond.

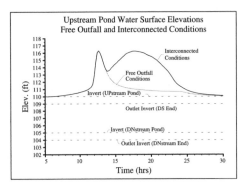

Figure 3-29: Elevations for upstream pond

Figure 3-30 compares the outflow from the upstream pond. The peak outflow rate was virtually unaffected since the peak elevation of the downstream pond did not coincide with the peak outflow of the upstream pond. For the interconnected scenario, there is a short period of reverse flow, and the total detention time is prolonged because of backwater effects.

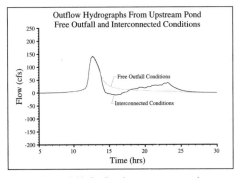

Figure 3-30: Outflow from upstream pond

Comparison for Downstream Pond

Figure 3-31 compares water surface elevations in the downstream pond. Notice the increased water surface elevation for the interconnected example. Both the maximum water surface and total detention time are greatly increased because of backwater effects from the river.

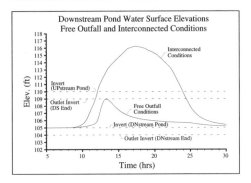

Figure 3-31: Elevations for downstream pond

Figure 3-32 compares outflow from the downstream pond. The interconnected backwater effects actually *reduce* the maximum outflow rate because of increased tailwater effects. Interconnected reverse flow also adds water to the downstream pond, thereby increasing the total storage volume and detention time in the downstream pond.

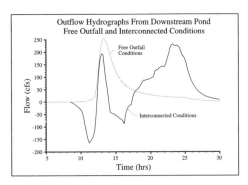

Figure 3-32: Outflow from downstream pond

Example 3: Flap Gates

This example is identical to Example 2, except that flap gates are modeled for both pond outlets in order to prevent reverse flow. The resulting water surface elevations and outflow rates are shown in Figure 3-33 and Figure 3-34.

Notice how the flap gates prevent reverse flow conditions and completely eliminate the outflow "spike" between hours 12 and 14 for the downstream pond (Figure 3-34). Since there is no reverse flow keeping the downstream pond's water surface near that of the river, the pond doesn't "catch up" to the river flood elevation during peak inflow (about 12 to 14 hours), thus preventing outflow until hour 20.

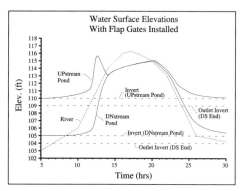

Figure 3-33: Elevations with flap gates

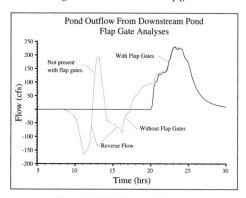

Figure 3-34: Outflow with flap gates

Flap gates in this case delay the outflow from the downstream pond, allowing them to occur only during the receding leg of the river flood stage.

Author: Michael K. Glazner

PondPack 6.0 software used for example computations and miscellaneous graphs.

Key Concepts

Here are a few rules of thumb to help you determine which routing technique is appropriate:

- Use standard routing techniques to calculate the maximum water surface elevation for each pond assuming they are not interconnected. If the maximum water surface elevation immediately downstream of each pond stays below the outfall invert, standard routing techniques apply. If the maximum water surface downstream of any pond rises above the outfall invert of the upstream connecting pond, interconnected analyses may be more appropriate.

- Time variant outfall elevations (such as ocean and river tides) require interconnected analyses if the TW elevation rises high enough to affect the pond outlet hydraulics. If the outfall TW is time variant but never rises high enough to affect the outflow rate of the connecting pond, standard routing techniques can be used.

- When in doubt, check the analyses using interconnected routing. If standard routing techniques apply, the interconnected results should compare closely to the standard routing results.

Interpreting SCS 24-Hour Storms

Understand how rainfall distributions impact your stormwater designs.

The U.S. Soil Conservation Service (SCS) 24-hour rainfall distributions (Types I, IA, II, and III) are some of the most widely used rainfall curves in the United States. This article explains the basic concept of a rainfall curve and discusses four SCS 24-hour distributions and how they impact hydrograph shape and peak flow rate.

The Basics

What is a rainfall curve?

A rainfall curve is the measure of total rainfall depth as it varies throughout a storm. A good way to understand a rainfall curve is to visualize the Y-axis as a rainfall gauge (see Figure 3-35). As the storm progresses, the gauge begins to fill. The curve describes the gauged rainfall depth at each point during the storm.

The steeper the curve's slope, the faster the gauge is filling. Hence, the rate of rainfall is more intense. In Figure 3-35, the most intense portion of the storm occurs between 0.1 and 0.2 hours and again between 0.5 and 0.6 hours (about 0.6" over 0.1 hour = 6"/hour intensity).

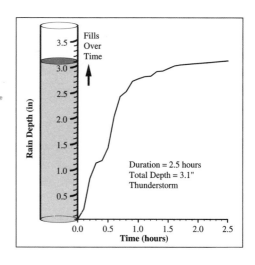

Figure 3-35: Gauged rainfall event

Rainfall curves are a mathematical means for simulating different storms. Figure 3-36 shows conditions for two types of storms. Figure 3-37 and Figure 3-38 display dramatic differences between these two rainfall events, even though the *total depth and volume are the same* for each storm.

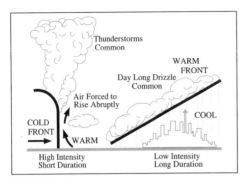

Figure 3-36: Conditions for two storms

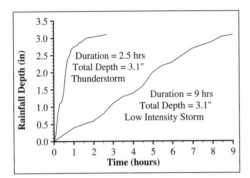

Figure 3-37: Comparison of two storms

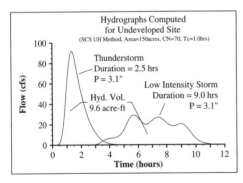

Figure 3-38: Hydrographs for two storms

The Diary of a Storm

A rainfall curve is a history, or "diary," of the recorded storm. Several pieces of information can be derived from rainfall curves:

- **Storm Duration** – Duration is the time between a storm's first and last raindrops. In Figure 3-35, the duration is 2.5 hours.

- **Total Depth** – Because the curve represents cumulative depth, the total depth (highest point) will be at the end of the storm. In Figure 3-35, the total depth is 3.1 inches.

- **Storm Intensity** – The slope of the line indicates the rainfall intensity as it varies throughout the storm. The steeper the line, the more intense (or "harder") the rainfall rate. In Figure 3-35, the most intense portions (about 6 inches per hour) of the storm are between 0.1 and 0.2 hours and between 0.5 and 0.6 hours.

- **Hydrograph Time to Peak** – When using the SCS unit hydrograph method, a *rough* rule of thumb for time to peak is:

$$T_P = T_{EI} + Lag, \text{ where:}$$
$$T_P = \text{Time to peak on hydrograph}$$
$$T_{EI} = \text{End of long, intense segment}$$
$$Lag = \text{Drainage lag (about } 0.6 \cdot T_C \text{ for SCS methods)}$$

In Figure 3-35, the end of the longest, most intense portion of the curve ends at about 0.7 hour. Therefore, the expected time to peak (for $T_C = 1.0$ hrs) would be about:

$$T_P = 0.7 + Lag = 0.7 + 0.6T_C$$
$$= 0.7 + (0.6)(1.0)$$

Expected T_P is about: 1.3 hours.
From Figure 3-38, the actual $T_P = 1.35$ hrs.

For natural rainfall curves there may be multiple inflection points that result in multiple "humps" on the hydrograph. (See 9-hour storm in Figure 3-37 and Figure 3-38).

- **Hydrograph Shape** – A steeper rainfall curve results in a higher peak discharge with a more "spiked" shape. A flatter rainfall curve yields a lower peak discharge with a more "rounded" shape.

- **Hydrograph Volume** – For runoff methods such as the SCS CN method, the *shape* of the rainfall curve does not affect total hydrograph *volume*. The total *depth* of rainfall impacts the total runoff volume. In Figure 3-38, the two hydrograph volumes are equal since each storm had the same total depth (applied to SCS methods).

Note: Some infiltration/runoff methods might result in runoff volumes that are a function of rainfall intensity (and therefore a function of the rain curve *shape*).

What are SCS 24-Hour Rainfall Curves?

Figure 3-39 displays four SCS distributions used in the United States (Types I, IA, II, and III). Figure 3-40 shows the approximate geographic boundaries for these rainfall distributions.

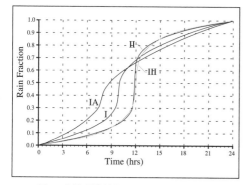

Figure 3-39: SCS 24-hour rainfall distributions

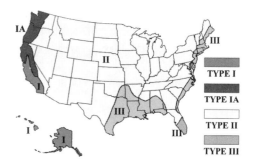

Figure 3-40: Approximate boundaries

Why Do We Need SCS Distributions?

Rainfall curves (not I-D-F curves) are needed for site designs that require hydrograph analyses (such as detention ponds, watershed studies, etc). Because local rainfall distribution curves have not been established for many areas in the United States, engineers often opt to use SCS distributions to compute hydrographs.

How Do SCS Distributions Model Storms?

The SCS distributions are dimensionless in their raw form (Figure 3-39). To create a design rainfall curve, multiply the Y-axis by the 24-hour total rainfall depth. Figure 3-41 shows what each distribution looks like when applied to a 24-hour total depth of 3.1 inches. Figure 3-42 displays hydrographs resulting from these distributions (applied to same site as Figure 3-38).

Comparison of Results

Figure 3-42 compares hydrographs computed using identical conditions for each scenario, changing only the shape and duration of the rainfall curve. The same total depth of 3.1 inches was used in each case and applied to the same site used for (Area=150 acres, CN=70 and Tc=1.0 hours). The SCS unit hydrograph procedure was used to compute the runoff hydrographs for each storm.

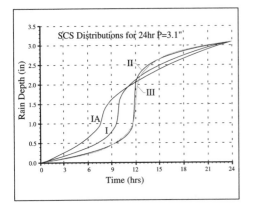

Figure 3-41: SCS distributions, 24-hour P=3.1"

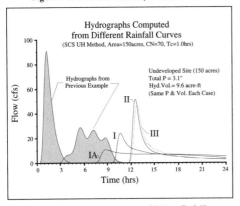

Figure 3-42: SCS hydrographs, 24-hour P=3.1"

This comparison shows that even for a given identical rainfall depth, the computed runoff hydrographs vary dramatically depending on the *shape and duration* of the rainfall curve. So before using any rainfall distribution, an engineer should understand the implied storm it represents.

Diary of the SCS 24-Hour Storm

An SCS dimensionless 24-hour rainfall distribution shares many of the same basic characteristics of a gauged storm event. Each SCS distribution provides a variety of information that will help you visualize the kind of storm it is modeling.

Here's a summary of important characteristics:

- **Storm Duration** – The SCS distributions in Figure 3-39 model only a 24-hour duration.

- **Total Depth** – Since the storm duration is 24 hours, the total depth applied to these distributions *must be for a 24-hour period.*

- **Why is the Y-axis dimensionless?** – The Y-axis is defined as fraction of total depth, ranging from 0 to 1.0 (0% to 100%). Multiply the Y-axis by total rainfall depth to "convert" the distribution to a rainfall depth curve.

  Defining the Y-axis as a *fraction* of total depth enables us to apply *different depths* to the same curve. The 24-hour rainfall depth varies with respect to storm *frequency* (2-year, 5-year, 25-year, etc), and *geographical region*.

- **Storm Intensity** – The steepest slope on a rainfall distribution represents the most intense portion of the storm. For the distributions in Figure 3-39, an intense period of rainfall is preceded and followed by several hours of lower-intensity rainfall.

  A range of average intensities can be computed for a rainfall curve, depending on the time "slice". Therefore, good judgment should be used in selecting the time step and location on the curve from which to compute the average intensity.

Figure 3-43 shows three examples for computing the average intensity for a portion of a rainfall curve. In these examples, the average intensities were computed for sections of the curve that had a relatively uniform slope.

Depth = 0.25" from <u>0 to 6 hrs</u>
Avg. Intensity = 0.25"/ 6 hrs = **0.04"/hr**

Depth = 0.96" from <u>11.7 to 12.0 hrs</u>
Avg. Intensity = 0.96"/0.3 hrs = **3.2"/hr**

Depth = 0.25" from <u>18 to 24 hrs</u>
Avg. Intensity = 0.25"/ 6hrs = **0.04"/hr**

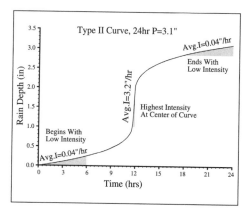

Figure 3-43: Average intensity examples

- **Hydrograph Time to Peak** – The time to peak on a hydrograph will usually occur after the longest, steepest (most intense portion) of the curve. In Figure 3-, the most intense portion for each SCS distribution ends at about:

Type IA – 8.2 hours
Type I – 10.0 hours
Type II – 12.0 hours
Type III – 12.2 hours

- From previous discussion, $T_P = T_{EI} + Lag$. For the Type II example in Figure 3-41, the expected time to peak is about:
$T_P = 12.0 + (0.6)(1.0) = 12.6$ hours.
Actual $T_P = 12.55$ hours (Figure 3-42).

Figure 3-42 includes the hydrographs computed for each of the SCS 24-hour rainfall curves. Note how each hydrograph peak time occurs after the long, steep (most intense) segment within the curve. Because there is only one inflection point on each SCS distribution, each resulting hydrograph has only one "hump."

- **Hydrograph Shape** – Figure 3-41 and Figure 3-42 show that as the slope of the rainfall distribution increases, the resulting hydrograph peak also increases. When comparing these SCS distributions, Type IA yields the least intense storms and Type II yields the most intense storms.

- **Hydrograph Volume** – For runoff methods such as the SCS CN method, the *shape* of the rainfall curve does not affect the total hydrograph *volume*. Only the total rainfall depth impacts runoff volume. So for the examples in Figure 3-42, the total hydrograph *volume* is identical in each case, even though the shapes are different.

Note: Some infiltration/runoff methods can result in runoff volumes that are a function of rainfall intensity (and therefore a function of the rain curve *shape*).

What Kinds of Storms Do They Simulate?

Center Peaking Storms

The SCS distributions (particularly Types II and III) can be described as center peaking storms. That is, the beginning and ends of the storms have a relatively low intensity compared to the middle portion's higher intensity.

A Closer Look

By "walking" along the rainfall distribution, we can better understand what kinds of storms these distributions model. Let's take a detailed look at the Type II distribution and visualize what kind of storm it models.

For the Type II storm in Figure 3-39, only 15% of total depth accumulates during the first 9 hours. About 70% of total depth falls in 6 hours (between 9 and 15 hours). The remaining 15% of total depth falls in about 9 hours. In other words, most of the rainfall accumulates in the center of the storm. In particular, about 40% falls in a 40-minute period (from 11.6 to 12.3 hours).

So the 24-hour Type II storm doesn't really model an intense storm that lasts for 24 hours. It models an intense storm of a few hours that is sandwiched between several hours of "drizzle" on each side.

Limitations

Although the SCS 24-hour rainfall distributions are readily available and easy to apply in the United States, they do have some limitations:

- **Regional Variation** – Figure 3-40 shows how each SCS distribution covers a large region of the United States. More studies

are needed to provide rainfall distributions for site-specific locations.

- **Only 24-hour Duration** – These SCS distributions are only for a 24-hour storm. More studies are needed to provide engineers with rainfall distributions for a wider variety of storm durations.

The Need

Only a handful of different SCS 24-hour rainfall distributions are applied across the entire United States. Studies are needed to provide engineers with more site-specific rainfall data for a wider range of durations (not just 24-hour).

Check with local and state drainage authorities to see if additional or newer rainfall curve data are available for your area.

Newer Rainfall Studies

Efforts are being made to better approximate rainfall curves for specific locations. Some areas in the United States now provide engineers with rainfall depths and distributions that replace or supplement the standard SCS 24-hour storms.

One example of updated rainfall information is found in the Illinois State Water Survey's Bulletin 70 (Huff et al, 1989), "Frequency Distributions and Hydroclimatic Characteristics of Heavy Rainstorms in Illinois." This document provides rainfall *depths* for a variety of return events and durations (not limited to 24 hours only). Bulletin 70 also provides rainfall distribution curves for a variety of durations. Additional discussion on the development of these dimensionless rainfall distributions is included in Circular 173, "Time Distributions of Heavy Rainstorms in Illinois," also by the Illinois State Water Survey.

Author: Michael K. Glazner

PondPack 6.0 software used for example computations and miscellaneous graphs.

Key Concepts

This article is designed to help engineers better understand SCS rainfall distributions. Here is a quick review of the topics discussed:

- How to read a gauged rainfall curve

- How to visualize an SCS rainfall distribution

- Comparing the differences between SCS distributions and gauged data

- How rainfall curves dramatically affect the shape of a hydrograph, even for the same total depth of rainfall

- Limitations of the 24-hour distributions

- The need for more research and rainfall information to be made available to practicing engineers

Rainfall Distributions:
Center-Peaking
vs. Statistical

---

*Identify various types of rainfall curves and
their underlying assumptions. They might
not be modeling quite what you think...*

Various types of rainfall distribution curves have been developed for use in hydrograph calculations. This article uses examples to demonstrate the differences between two major categories of rainfall curves: center peaking and statistically derived distributions.

Center Peaking Distribution

These types of rainfall curves are symmetrical in appearance and model storms in which the most intense (steepest slope on curve) portion of the storm is located near the center of the curve. Figure 3-44 is a classic example of a center peaking distribution. It shows the SCS 24-hour Type II rainfall distribution with a total depth of 3.1 inches applied.

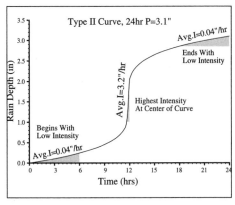

Figure 3-44: Type II 24-hour rainfall curve

This Type II rainfall distribution models an intense "thunderstorm" preceded and followed by periods of much lesser intensity. The article titled "Interpreting SCS 24-Hour Storms" provides detailed discussion on visualizing and understanding rainfall curves.

Other examples of center peaking distributions are those created from I-D-F curves. Different duration storms can be created using a single I-D-F curve (for one frequency).

The table in Figure 3-45 shows depth vs. duration data established in a recent rainfall study for a certain area in the United States. The I-D-F curve for the 10-year frequency was fit through the intensity points derived in the table.

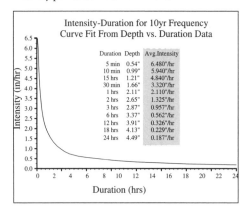

Figure 3-45: Intensity-Duration-Frequency

Figure 3-46 represents the rainfall distributions for various durations. These rainfall curves were created from the I-D-F curve in Figure 3-45.

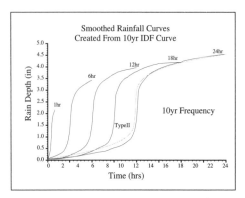

Figure 3-46: Rainfall curves created from I-D-F

Note that the *intensity* (slope) of the center portion of each curve created from I-D-F data is *identical* (for the same frequency). That is, the beginning and end "tails" of the same curve were lengthened to attain the desired duration and corresponding total depth.

These types of curves indicate that the most intense portions of the storms are the same, regardless of storm duration. This concept differs from the statistical distributions described below.

Statistical Distribution

These rainfall curve distributions are developed based on statistical analyses of storm events for different durations. When developed properly for a specific location, these types of rainfall distributions provide the flexibility of modeling a variety of storms other than the standard 24-hour event.

Statistical distributions are not necessarily center peaking and might have different maximum intensities compared to center peaking distributions.

The basic philosophy of this approach is that longer-duration storms are expected to "behave" differently than shorter-duration storms. For example, the most intense portion of a 24-hour storm is expected to differ from the most intense portion of a 1-hour storm.

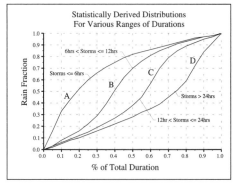

Figure 3-47: Statistical distributions

Typically, these types of curves are dimensionless, so they can be applied to a wide range of durations and rainfall depths.

Figure 3-47 displays dimensionless rainfall curves established for different ranges of durations. To create a rainfall depth curve, select the curve for the desired duration. Then, multiply the X-axis by total storm duration and multiply the Y-axis by the total rainfall depth for that given duration.

Example

Statistical analyses were performed using updated rainfall information for a certain geographic location in the United States. This study yielded the table shown in Figure 3-45 and the statistical distributions shown in Figure 3-47.

Given: Rainfall depths from Figure 3-45.

Find: Rainfall curves for the 1-, 6-, 12-, 18- and 24-hour durations, using the statistically derived distributions in Figure 3-47.

Solution: First, select the distribution from Figure 3-47 that corresponds to each desired duration. Then multiply the Y-axis by the total rainfall depth for that duration and the X-axis by that duration. Figure 3-48 displays the results of this example. Different curve types (A, B and C from) were used

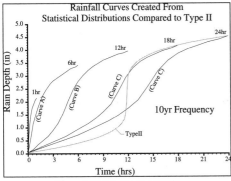

Figure 3-48: Solution to example

to model different duration storms. Note how the total depth increases, but overall intensity (slope of the curve) decreases as the duration is lengthened.

Implementation

One example of the statistical approach is found in the Illinois State Water Survey's Bulletin 70, "Frequency Distributions and Hydroclimatic Characteristics of Heavy Rainstorms in Illinois." This document provides rainfall depths for a variety of return events and durations (not just 24 hours).

Bulletin 70 also provides rainfall distribution curves for a variety of durations. Additional discussion on the development of these dimensionless rainfall distributions is included in Circular 173 (Huff, 1990), "Time Distributions of Heavy Rainstorms in Illinois," also issued by the Illinois State Water Survey.

By coupling the total depth for different durations and return events, these reports provide engineers with a wide range of design storms (for Illinois). And because the dimensionless rainfall curves cover a wide range of durations, engineers can develop a complete rainfall vs. depth curve for any of the included durations and return events.

Comparisons

24-Hour Duration Storms

Figure 3-49 compares 24-hour rainfall curves for a geographical area where the Type II rainfall curve is applicable. Three types of distributions are compared: a center peaking rainfall distribution; SCS Type II 24 hour; and a statistically derived rainfall curve.

The Type II and center peaking distribution are similar in shape. Conversely, the statistically derived distribution has an overall more uniform and lower intensity (milder slope) than the two center peaking storms.

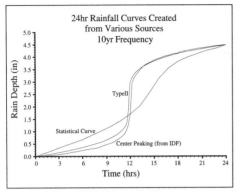

Figure 3-49: 24-hour rainfall curves

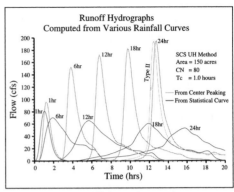

Figure 3-51: Hydrograph comparisons

Various Durations

Figure 3-50 directly compares the rainfall curves from Figure 3-46 and Figure 3-48 . Note how center peaking distributions have the same maximum intensity in the center of the storm for each duration, compared to the statistically derived distributions where maximum intensity tends to decrease with an increase in storm duration.

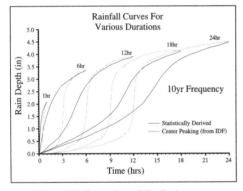

Figure 3-50: Comparison of distribution types

Figure 3-51 compares the hydrographs computed with these rainfall curves, using the same watershed data for each calculation. The center peaking distributions yield hydrographs that increase in peak discharge with an increase in duration. The statistically derived distributions, on the other hand, yield hydrographs that decrease in peak discharge with an increase in duration.

In each case, an increase in duration yields a higher total hydrograph volume since the total depth of rainfall increases with duration.

Total Volume

Runoff volume is only a function of total rainfall depth and runoff coefficient when using procedures such as the SCS Runoff CN method. As duration increases, the total volume increases because there is an increase in total depth of rainfall.

However, the hydrograph volume for each duration (same rainfall depth) is identical for both center peaking and statistically derived distributions, even though the hydrograph shapes are dramatically different.

Case Studies

Which is better?

As we have seen, there can be huge variations between center peaking and statistically derived distributions. Which one best models or predicts "real world" events?

Some people might argue that statistically derived rainfall distributions for a specific area would better represent the overall "average" shape of rainfall curves for different duration storm events. However, even if this assumption could be proved to be true, eventually rainfall events will still occur that significantly differ from the statistically calculated rainfall curves.

Maybe the question should be reworded to ask: "What type of storm is most appropriate for your design?" In other words, would a storm with a more uniform intensity or one with center peaking high intensity have the most significant impact on your design?

In the field, drainage facilities will encounter hundreds of variations of duration and intensity. Rarely will a site encounter two storms with identical duration, depth and rainfall curve shape.

By understanding the kinds of storms various rainfall distributions model, engineers can better judge their applicability for design situations. Engineers might want to model a system using more than one duration and/or type of rainfall distribution. By doing so, a design's response can be checked for greatly varying rainfall conditions.

Case Study: The Need for More Curves

A large event (7.76 inches over 19 hours) was recorded at a particular gauging station in the Eastern United States. The Type III 24-hour distribution is normally applied to this geographic location.

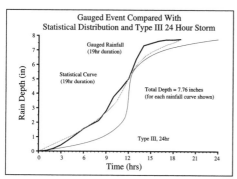

Figure 3-52: Gauged vs. Synthetic data

Figure 3-52 compares the actual gauged storm with a statistically derived distribution for the same duration and total rainfall depth. The 24-hour Type III storm is also compared using the same total rainfall depth.

For this particular event, the gauged data show an overall more uniform and lower intensity than the Type III 24-hour event. The statistically derived 19-hour distribution appears to better approximate the actual event than does the center peaking 24-hour Type III distribution.

This storm represents only a single historic event at this geographic location. Even though the engineer may consider the statistically derived distribution relevant for this case study, an actual event of this same magnitude will someday impact the design site, but can not be expected to match this same rainfall distribution assumption.

Figure 3-53 compares a hydrograph computed using the real gauged data to hydrographs computed from two different synthetic rainfall distributions (using the same total depth of 7.76 inches).

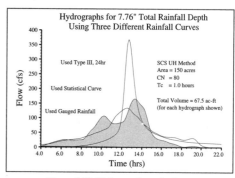

Figure 3-53: Hydrograph results from gauged and synthetic data

Another way to review the comparison would be to say the hydrograph from the Type III storm is the one the engineer used for design, while the gauged rainfall event is the one that actually occurred.

In this case study, is the Type III hydrograph conservative compared to the gauged event? The answer depends on the design situation.

If only one uniform subarea is being analyzed, and the outfall structure is designed *only* for *peak* discharge rate, the Type III storm would be conservative.

However, for more complex systems, such as detention ponds or watershed networks, the comparisons become more difficult. In order to assess the effectiveness of rainfall design assumptions, the entire system should be analyzed for *both* pre- and post-developed conditions using both gauged rainfall data and synthetic design distributions.

In this particular case, a statistically derived rainfall curve produces a closer (but not perfect) approximation of the actual gauged event. This case study shows why more research is needed to provide practicing drainage engineers with a much wider range of design rainfall distributions.

Author: Michael K. Glazner

PondPack 6.0 software used for example computations and miscellaneous graphs.

Key Concepts

This article discusses two distinctly different approaches to modeling rainfall curves: center peaking, and statistically derived distributions. Here is a review of the topics covered:

- Definition and examples of center peaking distributions

- Definition and examples of statistically derived distributions

- Comparisons of these two types of rainfall distributions and their significant differences in storm intensity

- Discussion of the dramatic differences between the hydrographs resulting from each type of rainfall distribution

- Case studies comparing real gauged data with center peaking and statistically based rainfall distributions

- Discussion of the need for more research and better rainfall models

---

Gauged Rainfall Source

Rainfall and other meteorological data from across the United States and around the world are compiled and archived at the National Climatic Data Center. This agency has daily precipitation depths and in some cases hourly precipitation data.

National Climatic Data Center
151 Patton Ave., Room 120
Federal Building
Asheville, NC 28801-5001

Phone: (704) 271-4800
Internet: www.ncdc.noaa.gov

Computational Differences and Results Interpretation of Common Water Surface Profiling Applications

Understand the differences between HEC-RAS and HEC-2 and make sense of the common error messages.

Part I: Computational Differences

HEC-RAS is a completely new software product. None of the computational routines in the HEC-2 program were used in the HEC-RAS software. When HEC-RAS was being developed, a significant effort was spent on improving the computational capabilities over those in the HEC-2 program. Because of this, there are computational differences between the two programs. The following describes all of the major areas in which computational differences can occur.

Cross Section Conveyance Calculations

Both HEC-RAS and HEC-2 utilize the Standard Step method for balancing the energy equation to compute a water surface for a cross section. A key element in the solution of the energy equation is the calculation of conveyance. The conveyance is used to determine friction losses between cross sections, the flow distribution at a cross section, and the velocity weighing coefficient alpha. The approach used in HEC-2 is to calculate conveyance between every coordinate point in the cross section overbanks (Figure 3-54). The conveyance is then summed to get the total left overbank and right overbank values. HEC-2 does

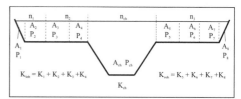

Figure 3-54: HEC-2 conveyance subdivision

not subdivide the main channel for conveyance calculations. This method of computing overbank conveyance can lead to different amounts of total conveyance when additional points are added to the cross section, with out actually changing the geometry. The HEC-RAS program supports this method for calculating conveyance, but the default method is to make conveyance calculations only at n-value break points (Figure 3-55).

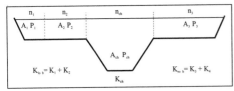

Figure 3-55: HEC-RAS default conveyance subdivision method.

Testing Using HEC-2 Conveyance Calculation Approach

Comparisons of HEC-RAS results with those from HEC-2 were performed using 97 data sets from the HEC profile accuracy study (HEC, 1986). Water surface profiles were computed for 10% and 1% chance floods using HEC-2 and HEC-RAS, both programs using the HEC-2 approach for computing overbank conveyance. Table 3-6 shows the percentage, of approximately 2000 cross sections, within +/- 0.02 feet (+/- 6 mm). For the 10% chance flood, 53 cross sections had differences greater than +/- 0.02 feet (6 mm). For those sections, 62.2% were caused by differences in computation of critical depth and 34% resulted from propagation of the difference upstream. For the 1% chance flood, 88 sections had elevation differences over +/- 0.02 feet (6 mm), of which 60.2% resulted from critical depth and 36.4% from the upstream propagation of downstream differences. HEC-RAS uses 0.01 feet (3 mm) for the critical depth error criterion, while HEC-2 uses 2.5% of the depth of flow.

Testing Using HEC-RAS and HEC-2 Approach

The two methods for computing conveyance will produce different answers whenever portions of the overbanks have ground sections with significant vertical slopes. In general, the HEC-RAS default approach will provide a lower total conveyance for the same elevation and, therefore, a higher computed water surface elevation. In order to test the significance of the two ways of computing conveyance, comparisons were performed using the same 97 data sets. Water surface profiles were computed for the 1% chance event using the two methods for computing conveyance in HEC-RAS. The results confirmed that the HEC-RAS default approach will generally produce a higher computed water surface elevation. Out of the 2048 cross section locations, 47.5% had computed water surface elevations within 0.10 feet (30.5 mm), 71 % within 0.20 feet (61 mm), 94.4% within 0.40 feet (122 mm), 99.4% within 1.0 feet (305 mm), and one cross section had a difference of 2.75 feet (0.84 m). Because the differences tend to be in the same direction, some effects can be attributed to propagation.

The results from these comparisons do not show which method is more accurate, they only show differences. In general, it is felt that the HEC-RAS default method is more commensurate with the Manning equation and the concept of separate flow elements. The default method in HEC-RAS is also more consistent, in that the computed conveyance is based on the geometry, and not on how many points are used in the cross section. Further research, with observed water surface profiles, will be needed to make any final conclusions about the accuracy of the two methods.

Difference (feet)	-0.02	-0.01	0.0	0.01	0.02	Total
10% Chance Flood	0.8%	11.2%	73.1%	11.2%	0.6%	96.9%
1% Chance Flood	2.0%	11.6%	70.1%	10.8%	1.3%	95.8%

Table 3-6: Computed water surface elevation difference (HEC-RAS - HEC-2)

Critical Depth Calculations

During the water surface profile calculations, each of the two programs may need to calculate critical depth at a cross section if any of the following conditions occur:

1) The supercritical flow regime has been specified by the user.

2) The calculation of critical depth has been requested by the user.

3) The current cross section is an external boundary cross section and critical depth must be determined to ensure the user-entered boundary condition is in the correct flow regime.

4) The Froude number check for a subcritical profile indicates that critical depth needs to be determined to verify the flow regime of the computed water surface elevation.

5) The program could not balance the energy equation within the specified tolerance before reaching the maximum number of iterations.

The HEC-RAS program has two methods for calculating critical depth: a "parabolic" method and a "secant" method. The HEC-2 program has one method, which is very similar to the HEC-RAS "parabolic" method. The parabolic method is computationally faster, but it is only able to locate a single minimum energy. For most cross sections there will only be one minimum on the total energy curve; therefore, the parabolic method has been set as the default method for HEC-RAS (the default method can be changed from the user interface). If the parabolic method is tried and it does not converge, then the HEC-RAS program will automatically try the secant method. The HEC-RAS version of the parabolic method calculates critical depth to a numerical accuracy of 0.01 feet, while HEC-2's version of the parabolic method

calculates critical depth to a numerical accuracy of 2.5 percent of the flow depth. This, in its self, can lead to small differences in the calculation of critical depth between the two programs.

In certain situations it is possible to have more than one minimum on the total energy curve. Multiple minimums are often associated with cross sections that have breaks in the total energy curve. These breaks can occur due to very wide and flat overbanks, as well as cross sections with levees and ineffective flow areas. When the parabolic method is used on a cross section that has multiple minimums on the total energy curve, the method will converge on the first minimum that it locates. This approach can lead to incorrect estimates of critical depth, in that the returned value for critical depth may be the top of a levee or an ineffective flow elevation. When this occurs in the HEC-RAS program, the software automatically switches to the secant method. The HEC-RAS secant method is capable of finding up to three minimums on the energy versus depth curve. Whenever more than one minimum energy is found, the program selects the lowest valid minimum energy (a minimum energy at the top of a levee or ineffective flow elevation is not considered a valid critical depth solution).

Given that HEC-RAS has the capability to find multiple critical depths, and detect possible invalid answers, the final critical depth solutions between HEC-2 and HEC-RAS could be quite different. In general the critical depth answer from the HEC-RAS program will always be more accurate than HEC-2.

Bridge Hydraulic Computations

A vast amount of effort has been spent on the development of the new bridge routines used in the HEC-RAS software. The bridge routines in HEC-RAS allow the modeler to analyze a bridge by several different methods with the same bridge geometry. The model utilizes four user defined cross sections in the computations of energy losses due to the structure. Cross sections are automatically formulated inside the bridge on an as need basis by combining the bridge geometry with the two cross sections that bound the structure. The HEC-2 program requires the user to use one of two possible methods, the special bridge routine or the normal bridge routine. The data requirements for the two methods are different, and therefore, the user must decide aprior which method to use.

Differences between the HEC-2 and HEC-RAS bridge routines will be addressed by discussing the two HEC-2 bridge methodologies separately.

HEC-2 Special Bridge Methodology

The largest computational differences will be found when comparing the HEC-2 special bridge routines to the equivalent HEC-RAS bridge methodologies. The following is a list of what is different between the two programs:

1) The HEC-2 special bridge routines use a trapezoidal approximation for low flow calculations [**editors note:** except for bridge openings that do not have piers] (Yarnell equation and class B flow check with the momentum equation). The HEC-RAS program uses the actual bridge opening geometry for all of the low flow methodologies.

2) Also for low flow, the HEC-2 program uses a single pier (of equivalent width to the sum total width of all piers) placed in the middle of the trapezoid. In the HEC-RAS software, all of the piers are defined separately, and the hydraulic computations are performed by evaluating the water surface and impact on each pier individually. While this is more data for the user to enter, the results are much more physically based.

3) For pressure flow calculations, HEC-2 requires the net flow area of the bridge opening. The HEC-RAS software calculates the area of the bridge opening from the bridge and cross section geometry. Because of the potential error involved in calculating the bridge opening area by hand, differences between the programs may occur for pressure flow calculations.

4) The HEC-RAS software has two equations that can be used for pressure flow. The first equation is for a fully submerged condition (i.e. when both the upstream side and downstream side of the bridge is submerged). The fully submerged equation is also used in HEC-2. A second equation is available in HEC-RAS, which is automatically applied when only the upstream side of the bridge is submerged. This equation computes pressure flow as if the bridge opening were acting as a sluice gate. The HEC-2 program only has the fully submerged pressure flow equation. Therefore, when only the upstream side of the bridge is submerged, the two programs will compute different answers for pressure flow because they will be using different equations.

5) When using the HEC-2 special bridge routines, it is not necessary for the user to specify low chord information in the bridge table (BT data). The bridge table information is only used for weir flow in HEC-2. When HEC-2 special bridge data is imported into HEC-RAS, the user must enter the low chord information in order to define the bridge opening. This is due to the fact that the trapezoidal approximation used in HEC-2 is not used in HEC-RAS, and therefore the opening must be completely defined.

6) When entering bridge table (BT records) information in the HEC-2 special bridge method, the user had to enter stations that followed along the ground in the left overbank, then across the bridge deck/road embankment; and then along the ground of the right overbank. This was necessary in order for the left and right overbank area to be used in the weir flow calculations. In HEC-RAS this is not necessary. The bridge deck/roadway information only needs to reflect the additional blocked out area that is not part of the ground. HEC-RAS will automatically merge the ground information and the high chord data of the bridge deck/roadway.

HEC-2 Normal Bridge Methodology

In general, when importing HEC-2 normal bridge data into HEC-RAS there should not be any problems. The program automatically selects the energy based methods for low flow and high flow conditions, which is equivalent to the normal bridge method. The following is a list of possible differences that can occur.

1) In HEC-2 pier information is either entered as part of the bridge table (BT data) or the ground information (GR data). If the user stays with the energy based methods in HEC-RAS the results should be about the same. If the user wishes to use either the Momentum or Yarnell methods for low flow, they must first delete the pier information from the BT or GR data, and then re-enter it as separate pier information in HEC-RAS. If this is not done, HEC-RAS will not know about the pier information, and will therefore incorrectly calculate the losses with either Momentum or Yarnell methods.

2) The HEC-2 Normal bridge method utilizes six cross sections. HEC-RAS uses only four cross sections in the vicinity of the bridge. The two cross sections inside the bridge are automatically formulated from the cross sections outside the bridge and the bridge geometry. In general, it is common for HEC-2

users to repeat cross sections through the bridge opening (i.e. the cross sections used inside the bridge were a repeat of the downstream section). If however, the HEC-2 user entered completely different cross sections inside the bridge than outside, the HEC-RAS software will add two additional cross sections just outside of the bridge, in order to get the correct geometry inside of the bridge. This however gives the HEC-RAS data set two more cross sections than the original HEC-2 data set. The two cross sections are placed at zero distance from the bridge, but could still cause some additional losses due to contraction and expansion of flow. The user may want to make some adjustments to the data when this happens.

3) In HEC-2 the stationing of the bridge table (BT Records) had to match stations on the ground (GR data). This is not required in HEC-RAS. The stationing of the data that makes up a bridge (ground, deck/roadway, piers, and abutments) does not have to match in any way, HEC-RAS will interpolate any points that it needs.

Culvert Hydraulic Computations

The culvert routines in HEC-RAS and HEC-2 were adapted from the Federal Highway Administrations Hydraulic Design of Highway Culverts publication, HDS No. 5 (FHWA, 1985). The following is a list of the differences between the two programs.

1) HEC-2 can only perform culvert calculations for box and circular culvert shapes. HEC-RAS can handle the following shapes: box, circular pipe, semi-circle, arch, pipe arch, vertical ellipse, horizontal ellipse, low profile arch, and high profile arch.

2) HEC-RAS also has the ability to mix the culvert shapes, sizes, and all other parameters at any single culvert crossing. In HEC-2 the user is limited to the same shape and size barrels.

Floodway Encroachment Computations

The floodway encroachment capabilities in HEC-RAS were adapted from those found in HEC-2. For the most part encroachment methods 1-3 in HEC- RAS are the same as methods 1-3 in HEC-2. The following is a list of the differences between the two programs.

1) HEC-RAS has an additional capability of allowing the user to specify a left and right encroachment offset. While in general the encroachments can go all the way up to the main channelbank stations, the offset establishes an additional buffer zone around the main channel bank stations for limiting the encroachments. The offset is applicable to methods 2-5 in HEC-RAS.

2) The logic of method 4 in HEC-RAS is the same as method 4 in HEC- 2. The only difference is that the HEC-RAS method 4 will locate the final encroachment to an accuracy of 0.01 feet while the HEC-2 method 4 uses a parabolic interpolation method between the existing cross section points. Since conveyance is non-linear with respect to the horizontal stationing, the interpolation in HEC-2 does not always find the encroachment station as accurately as HEC-RAS.

3) Method 5 in HEC-RAS is a combination of HEC-2's methods 5 and 6. The HEC-RAS method five can be used to optimize for a change in water surface (HEC-2 method 5); a

change in energy (HEC-2 method 6); or both parameters at the same time (new feature).

4) At bridges and culverts, the default in HEC-RAS is to perform the encroachment, while in HEC-2 the default was not to perform the encroachment. Both programs have the ability to turn encroachments at bridges and culverts on or off.

5) At bridges where the energy based modeling approach is being used (similar to HEC-2's normal bridge method), HEC-RAS will calculate the encroachment for each of the cross sections through the bridge individually. HEC-2 will take the encroachments calculated at the downstream side of the bridge and fix those encroachment stations the whole way through the bridge.

6) In HEC-2, if the user specifies a fixed set of encroachments on the X3 record, this would override anything on the ET record. In HEC-RAS, when the data is imported the X3 record encroachment is converted into a blocked obstruction. Therefore any additional encroachment information found on the ET record will be used in addition to the blocked obstruction.

New Computational Features in HEC-RAS

The following is a list of new computational features found in HEC-RAS that are not available in HEC-2.

1) HEC-RAS can perform subcritical, supercritical, or mixed flow regime calculations all in a single execution of the program. The cross section order does not have to be reversed (as in HEC-2), the user simply presses a single button to select the computational flow regime. When in a mixed flow regime mode, HEC-RAS can also locate hydraulic jumps.

2) HEC-RAS has the ability to perform multiple bridge and/or culvert openings at the same road crossing.

3) At bridges, the user has the ability to use a momentum based solution for class A, B, and C low flow. In HEC-2 the momentum equation was used for class B and C flow, and requires the trapezoidal approximation. The HEC-RAS momentum solution also takes into account friction and weight forces that HEC-2 does not.

4) HEC-RAS can model single reaches, dendritic stream systems, or fully looped network systems. HEC-2 can only do single reaches and a limited number of tributaries (up to three stream orders).

5) At stream junctions, HEC-RAS has the ability to perform the calculations with either an energy based method or a momentum based method. HEC-2 only has the energy based method.

6) HEC-RAS has the following new cross section properties not found in HEC-2: blocked ineffective flow areas; normal ineffective flow areas can be located at any station (in HEC-2 they are limited to the main channel bank stations); blocked obstructions; and specification of levees.

7) In HEC-RAS the user can enter up to 500 points in a cross section. HEC-2 has a limit of 100.

8) HEC-RAS has the ability to perform geometric cross section interpolation. HEC-2 interpolation is based on a ratio of the current cross section and a linear elevation adjustment.

9) HEC-RAS has an improved flow distribution calculation routine. The new routine can subdivide the main channel as well as the overbanks, and the user has control over how many subdivisions are used. The HEC-2 flow distribution option is limited to the overbank areas and breaks at existing coordinate points.

Reprinted from the US Army Corps of Engineers <u>Hydraulic Reference Guide</u> *for HEC-RAS.*

Part II: Interpreting the Results

Consider a community that participates in the Federal Emergency Management Agency's National Flood Insurance Program. Chances are that FEMA maps have already been developed for all flood-prone areas within the community. Consequently, if one wishes to place a development adjacent to a stream that has been mapped, the engineer is responsible for ensuring that the development does not cause water surface elevations to increase. In fact, assurances should be made that a development situated next to a stream does not cause any adverse impact on the stream regardless of whether it has been mapped or not. The most common means of gauging the effect of development on water surface profiles is to use either the HEC-2 or HEC-RAS computer program.

HEC-2 is a venerable engineering model that has been in widespread use for over 30 years. HEC-RAS, on the other hand, is the new kid on the block, having been released during the summer of 1995. While HEC-2 is a DOS-based program, HEC-RAS operates in the Windows environment. However, HEC-RAS is more than just a Windows version of HEC-2. HEC-RAS has several hydraulic features that are not found in HEC-2, including improved bridge and culvert modeling,

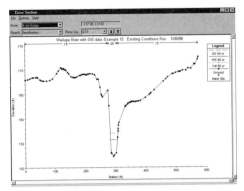

Figure 3-56: A typical river cross-section in HEC-RAS

momentum-based junction analysis and multiple opening analysis. Be careful when using HEC-RAS to reproduce HEC-2 output, though. Unless told to do otherwise, the two models will compute cross-section conveyances differently.

Warnings and Errors

No matter if the HEC-2 or HEC-RAS application involves determining floodways, evaluating bridges or just finding the water surface elevation associated with a particular flood event, certain warning messages will almost certainly be present in your output files. In fact, experienced HEC-2 users will guarantee that the following messages almost always find their way into any water surface profiling project:

3685 20 TRIALS ATTEMPTED WSEL,CWSEL

3693 PROBABLE MINIMUM SPECIFIC ENERGY

3720 CRITICAL DEPTH ASSUMED

3302 WARNING: CONVEYANCE CHANGE OUTSIDE OF ACCEPTABLE RANGE, KRATIO = X.XX

3301 HV CHANGED MORE THAN HVINS

Although the presence of these messages can be aggravating, they do not necessarily represent a numerical kiss of death. In fact, one may consider these messages to really be warnings and not errors since HEC-2 and HEC-RAS will successfully complete a simulation even though the messages are present. It is important, however, that the modeler be aware of exactly what these messages mean. Armed with this knowledge, the modeler can then take appropriate steps to address these messages in proper fashion.

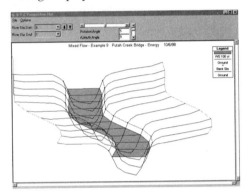

Figure 3-57: HEC-RAS x-y-z perspective

20 Trials Attempted

HEC-2 and HEC-RAS compute water surface elevations by balancing the energy equation between two adjacent cross-sections. With the water surface elevation at one of the cross-sections known, the water surface elevation at the other cross-section is computed. Once the unknown water surface elevation has been found, the energy equation is balanced for another pair of cross-sections. However, this time the water level that was just found becomes the known water surface elevation. Computations proceed in this manner until the water surface elevation at all cross-sections has been computed.

The energy equation is solved in an iterative fashion until the computed water surface elevation agrees with an assumed water surface elevation within a given tolerance over a given number of iterations. In HEC-2, the tolerance is 0.01 feet (meters) and the maximum number of iterations is 20. HEC-RAS allows certain model tolerances to be changed, including the convergence tolerance criteria and the maximum number of iterations.

If the energy equation can not balance within 20 iterations, HEC-2 will then set the computed water surface elevation equal to critical depth and water surface profile computations will proceed as before. But caution: What this means is that for the next pair of cross-sections, the known water surface elevation is equal to critical depth when the actual water level in the stream under the specified discharge may not be at critical depth. In other words, the model was simply unable to balance the energy equation.

HEC-RAS behaves a little differently. While the iterations are taking place for a given set of cross-sections, HEC-RAS stores the difference between the assumed and computed water surface elevations. If the energy equation can not be balanced within the specified number of iterations (40 maximum for HEC-RAS), HEC-RAS checks the value of the smallest difference between assumed and computed water levels. If this value is less than a specified tolerance, HEC-RAS uses the computed water surface elevation associated with the smallest difference. If the smallest difference is larger than the specified tolerance, HEC-RAS sets the computed water surface elevation equal to critical depth just like HEC-2.

There are several reasons why the energy equation can not be balanced within the maximum number of iterations. One reason is that the distance between cross-sections might be too large. More likely, however, the geometry of the cross-section where the water surface is being computed is very sensitive to changes in water level.

Conveyance Change Outside Acceptable Range

A very common warning message encountered in HEC-2 and HEC-RAS simulations is the message dealing with conveyance changes – more commonly known as the conveyance ratio. Both programs compute friction losses in the reach between cross-sections by multiplying the reach length by an average friction slope. The friction slope at each cross-section is found using the conveyance of the section. Both programs offer four approaches to computing the average friction slope.

The conveyance is a measure of the carrying capacity of the stream. As the conveyance decreases, the friction slope increases. The friction slope can be thought of as the amount of energy needed to force a specified discharge through a cross-section having a given conveyance. Ideally, when computing the average friction slope the conveyance of each cross-section and hence the friction slope at each section should be roughly the same. If the conveyance of one cross-section is much lower than the conveyance of the adjacent section, the section with the lower conveyance (higher friction slope) can dominate the friction loss term. This may not accurately reflect the actual friction loss between cross-sections. HEC-2 and HEC-RAS will give the conveyance ratio warning when the ratio of conveyances between any two cross-sections is outside the range of 0.7 to 1.4.

The easiest, albeit most costly, way to address this message is to add cross-sections such that the hydraulic characteristics between any two adjacent cross-sections are fairly uniform. Recall that with surface profiling, a continuous water surface is being found using a series of discrete points, i.e. cross-sections. By increasing the number of cross-sections, one can more accurately model a true continuous profile. However, as the number of cross-sections is increased, the cost to obtain the cross-sectional geometry is also increased. Thus, the modeler must compromise by balancing the number of cross-sections with the cost of performing the analysis. Fortunately, the cross-section interpolation routine in HEC-RAS offers a low-cost means of gauging the effect of adding cross-sections.

Velocity Head Change More Than 0.5 Feet

As noted earlier, HEC-2 and HEC-RAS compute water surface elevations by balancing the energy equation between two adjacent cross-sections. As part of this process, the velocity head at each cross-section is computed. If the difference in velocity heads exceeds a specified value, a message to this effect is displayed. The allowable difference in velocity heads in HEC-2 and HEC-RAS is 0.5 feet.

There are several reasons why the difference in velocity heads is higher than allowed. Typically, this message will appear when there are rather significant changes in channel characteristics between two cross-sections – particularly the cross-sectional area. Again, recall that a continuous water surface profile is being modeled using a series of discrete points. The key in surface profiling is to select the location of cross-sections so that gradual changes in the hydraulic characteristics of a channel occur from cross-section to cross-section. It's also important that the channel characteristics associated with an individual cross-section be representative of the channel characteristics upstream and downstream of that cross-section.

Both models offer a means to test the effect of adding cross-sections by using interpolated cross-sections. HEC-2 inserts up to a maximum of three interpolated cross-sections between any two established sections based on the value of HVINS that is the variable in the 7th field of the J1 card. If the difference in velocity heads is greater than

HVINS, an interpolated cross-section is inserted. A maximum of three interpolated cross-sections per violation of HVINS will be used by HEC-2. The geometry of the interpolated section is taken from the established cross-sections.

HEC-RAS, on the other hand, allows an unlimited number of interpolated cross-sections to be included in the analysis. The number and location of the interpolated sections is based on a length that is specified by the modeler. By using interpolated cross-sections, the modeler can determine the number and location of any additional cross-sections that might need to be added. Interpolated cross-sections can also be used to help address problems with changes in conveyances and the inability of the energy equation to converge.

Reprinted from Haestad Press's 1997 Practical Guide to Hydraulics and Hydrology.

Author: Donald V. Chase, Ph.D., PE

HEC-2 and HEC-RAS software used for example computations, screen captures, and miscellaneous charts and graphs

References

American Association of State Highway and Transportation Officials (AASHTO). 1991. *AASHTO Model Drainage Manual.*

Brown, S.A., Stein S.M., and Warner J.C. 1996. *Urban Drainage Design Manual*, Hydraulic Engineering Circular Number 22, U.S. Department of Transportation, Federal Highway Administration, Washington, D.C.

Federal Highway Administration. 1985. *Hydraulic Design of Highway Culverts.* Hydraulic Design Series Number 5. U.S. Department of Transportation. Washington, D.C.

Haestad Press. 1997. *Practical Guide to Hydraulics and Hydrology.* Waterbury, CT: Haestad Press.

Huff, F. A., and Angel, J. R. 1989. *Frequency Distribution and Hydroclimatic Characteristics of Heavy Rainstorms in Illinois.* Bulletin 70. State of Illinois Department of Energy and Natural Resources. Champaign, IL.

Huff, F. A., and Angel, J. R. 1992. *Rainfall Frequency Atlas of the Midwest.* Bulletin 71. Midwestern Climate Center. Champaign, IL.

Huff, F.A. 1990. *Time Distributions of Heavy Rainstorms in Illinois.* Circular 173. State of Illinois Department of Energy and Natural Resources. Champaign, IL.

Hydrologic Engineering Center. 1986. Accuracy of Computed Water Surface Profiles. Research Document 26. US Army Corps of Engineers. Davis, CA.

Johnson, F. L., and Chang, F.F.M. 1984. *Drainage of Highway Pavements*, Hydraulic Engineering Circular Number 12, U.S. Department of Transportation, Federal Highway Administration, McLean, Virginia.

Business and Computers

Animation and Sound: Using Multimedia for Product Evaluation and Continuing Education

Open doors to valuable resources through multimedia.

Multimedia is the fusion of multiple technologies such as sound, text, graphics, animation, and video. Although many serious business applications now benefit from multimedia technologies, they often still carry an "entertainment" stigma. Thus, it's no surprise that some engineers feel almost guilty for running software applications with sound, since the implication is that it must be too much "fun" to be of any serious use. This article will explain why today's multimedia capabilities are more than just "fun and games", and in fact are fast becoming critical to a firm's productivity. Additionally, it will review multimedia hardware, software, and pricing, and discuss how these technologies have matured into useful tools for today's practicing civil engineers.

What is a Multimedia PC?

Companies often mistakenly think it is expensive to buy multimedia capable computers, even though top of the line sound cards only cost about $150. In fact, in newer PCs, sound chips are put directly onto the motherboard. It can cost more to get a mail order PC with disabled sound capabilities than a standard PC with a multimedia package.

The recommended requirements for a multimedia PC are a sound card, external speakers, and a CD-ROM drive. However, for fast, smooth multimedia it is recommended that the PC be at least a 300 MHz Pentium II or equivalent with an excellent sound card, self amplified speakers, 24x or faster CD-ROM drive, and 64MB of RAM. This type of PC configuration represents only a $1,000 investment as of October 1998.

How is Multimedia useful to Engineers Today?

Multimedia is already impacting civil engineering through Internet technologies, computer based training, and product comparisons. Let's look at these benefits in more detail...

How does Streaming Data Work?

Streaming media is an example of next generation Internet technology. Some companies, such as RealNetworks, have already introduced streaming media players that can receive audio and video media over the web.

Step 1: The media file is compressed and made available for downloading on a web page.

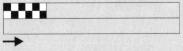

Step 2: When a user clicks on the media file in the web page the user's RealPlayer application program opens, and then starts to download a small portion of the media file. The player decompresses the first data packet and stores it in random access memory (RAM).

Step 3: Next, the player will simultaneously download, decompress, and store the next packet of data into a temporary file while the first downloaded packet is played.

Step 4: The player will repeat step 3 until the entire file has been played.

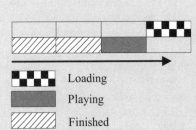

Loading

Playing

Finished

The player needs to be downloaded and installed before streaming video can be viewed (a one time installation). The program then resides on the user's computer and loads whenever a streaming video/audio file is accessed via the Internet.

To download the RealPlayer, go to: **http://www.real.com.**

For an example of a streaming video product demo, try the Haestad Methods Screening Room located at: **http://www.haestad.com/video/default.htm**

Internet Resources

The Internet has earned the name "Information Superhighway" for good reason — it has evolved into one of the fastest and most accessible information resources available. The increasingly complex technology on the Internet is demanding the same speed and complexity from the computers that are accessing it. For access to the full power of the Internet, a computer with excellent graphics and sound capabilities, comparable to those required by multimedia applications, is paramount.

For example, Internet resources such as streaming audio and video (see next page) require multimedia capabilities. Streaming audio and video allows a web site (such as the Haestad Methods Screening Room at **http://www.haestad.com/video** shown in Figure 4-1) to send a continuous stream

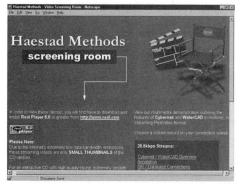

Figure 4-1: Haestad Methods Screening Room

of data to your web browser. This stream of data is then decoded by a program like RealPlayer, shown in Figure 4-2, and played in the form of audio and/or video on your PC. This technology can be used to view product demos, hear product testimonials, experience live news clips, or attend a virtual lecture or course presented on a relevant engineering topic.

Figure 4-2: Streaming video

Web-based training is another Internet technology that is growing rapidly and will be very useful to engineers. Web-based training allows an engineer to access a web page that uses Internet and multimedia technologies to provide education. The trainee can see, hear, and interact with a lesson transmitted from thousands of miles away. And since the lesson is on the web, it is accessible to engineers anywhere, at any time.

Multimedia Training

Multimedia is an excellent medium for training and learning tools. By incorporating sight and sound into an interactive lesson, multimedia tutorials, lessons and workshops create an environment that accelerates the learning process.

For example, some programs include tutorials to introduce the software using step by step examples in which text boxes explain each part of the process. Multimedia tutorials make this process an interactive experience that allows the engineer to listen to explanations, see graphical representations of abstract processes and theories, all while interacting with the tutorial at the same time. Because these events are occurring simultaneously, the brain learns at a more rapid pace than reading visual text and graphics in a linear fashion.

Another application of interactive multimedia learning is Computer Based Training (CBT). Currently, engineers can earn Continuing Education Units (CEUs) by attending workshops or doing exercises from a textbook. With multimedia CBT, engineers could earn CEUs from an interactive CD without missing a day at the office. Yet, the graphics, sound, and interaction bring the training close to the feeling of attending a live workshop.

A CBT application demonstrates concepts using graphics, animations, visual metaphors, and voice explanations. This simultaneous learning stimulation can exponentially increase learning speeds for the user. CBT lessons could have the same enhanced learning as multimedia tutorials, and the exercises could be repeated as many times as necessary. An engineer earning CEUs could do the exercises and/or tests directly on the CD and then mail in a file to be graded, or submit answers over the Internet. Earning CEUs could not be more convenient.

Product Demos

Powerful civil engineering software tools typically involve an initial investment of $2,000 to $10,000 for a single licensed seat. With a capital outlay of this magnitude, firms must be absolutely sure they select the best models on the market. The typical channels today for product information are printed brochures, faxed detail sheets, sales engineers, and Internet web sites. These are all valuable resources, but from these alone can you really get a "feel" for how the software works, or how easy it is to apply to your design conditions?

A well designed multimedia presentation, such as the Haestad Methods Water Distribution Modeling Demo displayed in Figure 4-3, will explain key features (using voice, graphics, and demonstrations), and summarize important capabilities. In just a few minutes, you will grasp a

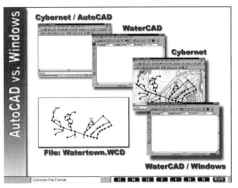

Figure 4-3: Water distribution modeling demonstration

distilled knowledge of the product that otherwise could only be obtained by spending several hours exploring every feature on a live project – after you have already bought it.

A "live" presentation of the software is one of the most effective ways to see how well the software is organized, and how intuitive the program is to use. Well designed multimedia demonstrations will allow the user to view the software in varying degrees of detail, allowing the engineer to select either a quick overview or an in-depth description of a feature depending on his or her level of interest (Figure 4-4). These capabilities add up to the fastest, most efficient, and most comprehensive review of the product's capabilities and ease of use.

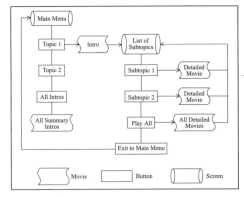

Figure 4-4: Varying degrees of detail

When a software company offers a cutting edge, multimedia presentation, it is demonstrating two important characteristics. First, they are using leading edge technology, which is a prerequisite to long term survival in the software industry. Second, they are interested in helping potential customers make informed decisions about buying their product. This demonstrates an interest in a long-term relationship rather than a quick sale. Providing quick and easy access to all of the necessary information saves time and money for prospective clients.

Why Multimedia?

Why should every engineer have a multimedia PC? Multimedia today is more than just "fun and games." This technology opens the door to valuable resources such as the Internet, interactive learning, and product reviews that can directly affect your organization's bottom line in real dollars. And best of all – the price is right.

Coauthors: Benjamin Ewing &
            Michael K. Glazner

Embrace
the Internet or Die
Revisited

*Civil engineering organizations that are not on the
Internet are running out of time.*

B ecause of the Internet's paramount importance in business today, we've decided to revamp and reprint this article from Haestad Press's <u>1997 Practical Guide to Hydraulics and Hydrology</u>. It is important to note that the information in this piece is even more relevant today than when it originally ran, so if you are reading it for the first time, take heed. If, however, you read the original and ignored our plea to "Embrace the Internet or Die!," we have just one question for you...Are you still alive?

Civil Engineering businesses that want to stay competitive and communicate effectively with clients, vendors and other agencies must have an open door to the Internet. In fact, it could be argued that having an Internet presence is the 90s equivalent to having a business listing in the yellow pages. More people are talking, communicating and doing business over the Internet everyday through email, discussion groups and Web pages. With the advent of affordable high-speed connectivity on the horizon for both the consumer and business markets in the form of Cable Modems, DSL (or Digital Subscriber Line), and Frame Relay, real-time audio and video transmissions will soon be commonplace as well.

If you have delayed your move to the Internet because of comments you've read or heard, you're probably pushing your luck. You must embrace the Internet now, before you lose your competitive advantage.

In this article, we provide an overview of the Internet. We'll give some practical advice on developing an Internet presence and exploiting the available technology. We'll also share some of our ideas and show you what other engineering organizations are doing. Let us help you learn from our own Internet experiences.

The Web Explosion

Two years ago, many industry analysts were cautioning against committing the resources necessary to join the fledgling Internet revolution. They said it was best to adopt a wait-and-see attitude and let the technology evolve.

The debate raged through 1995 and into 1996. Many skeptics said that the World Wide Web was just a fad destined to burn out and that people would come to believe that the Internet delivered no real value to the business world.

One widely published and respected industry pundit pronounced – with his characteristically acid-tipped pen – in early 1995:

> *Combine all the scenarios of time wasting, money wasting, information overload, Web hackers, and false promises and the Internet could take a serious tumble. We'll someday look back on the Internet sycophants and ask, "Gee, how did all those dinky companies make money?...The Internet probably should be completely shut down tomorrow for productivity reasons."*

—John Dvorak, "Info Overload at Your Fingertips," PC Magazine, March 28, 1995

But the Web was only beginning to emerge in the mainstream in 1995 and Dvorak's pronouncement then is in sharp contrast to his own statement made just over a year later:

> *Everyone should have a Web page. Why not? Unless you're living in a hole and want to stay there, Web pages are becoming so inexpensive that it's silly not to have one. With the upcoming Microsoft operating systems, it's actually going to be possible to put yourself on the Web with your own server, running one of those $20-per-month AT&T connections.*

—John Dvorak, "Isn't it About Time You Have Your Own URL", PC Magazine Online, July 9, 1996

What turned skeptics like John Dvorak into believers?

For one thing, five months after Dvorak's initial pronouncement, Netscape sky-rocketed into Wall Street after hosting the most successful stock launch the market has ever seen. Although we have had Web browsers such as Lynx and Mosaic since early 1992, they were by-and-large text only and initially available only on the Unix platforms. It wasn't until 1994 and the release of Netscape Navigator that the World Wide Web started to make its way into the mainstream and onto our collective desktops. Recently Netscape made waves throughout the Internet world by announcing that it's Communicator product would be available free-of-charge and that the source code would be made available to developers worldwide. In doing this, Netscape seems to be attempting to duplicate the success of such "open-source" projects as Linux (the most popular Unix "flavor") and Apache (the most used web server software on the Internet). The reasoning behind this decision can be found in this excerpt from the official press release:

> *MOUNTAIN VIEW, Calif. (January 22, 1998) - Netscape Communications Corporation (NASDAQ: NSCP) today announced bold plans to make the source code for the next generation of its highly popular Netscape Communicator client software available for free licensing on the Internet. The company plans to post the source code beginning with the first Netscape Communicator 5.0 developer release, expected by the end of the first quarter of 1998. This*

aggressive move will enable Netscape to harness the creative power of thousands of programmers on the Internet by incorporating their best enhancements into future versions of Netscape's software. This strategy is designed to accelerate development and free distribution by Netscape of future high-quality versions of Netscape Communicator to business customers and individuals, further seeding the market for Netscape's enterprise solutions and Netcenter business.

To support this effort, Netscape launched Mozilla.org (Figure 4-5) a point of central community for thousands of developers worldwide working collectively on improvements to the product including ports to other operating systems, add-ons, alternative interfaces and more.

Figure 4-5: Mozilla.org

After some initial, although short-lived, resistance, Microsoft jumped squarely into the Internet fray. Internet Explorer 4.0 is currently available for download on their Web site, and their corporate focus is set very clearly towards Internet integration with their complete product line. This past year, Microsoft found themselves in the middle of a nasty legal battle as several state Attorneys General leveled charges of antitrust issues. These charges focused on the release of Windows 98, which

tightly integrates the Internet Explorer browser with the users desktop.

Internet surfing has become a mainstream business activity. A look at Figure 4-6 shows that the number of Internet domain servers is growing exponentially, with no end in sight. A significant majority of the technical and political issues have now been answered and laid to rest. The Internet is here to stay, and the time for your organization to make the commitment is now.

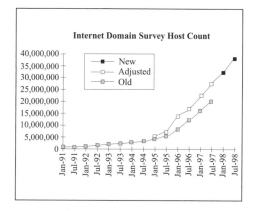

Figure 4-6: Internet domain servers

Internet Web Primer

"The Web" is a shorthand term for the World Wide Web. A web is an appropriate metaphor for this network of hyper-linked information pages, which in addition to text and images can also contain video and sounds. In fact, streaming technology by companies like Real Networks have made it possible to serve up audio and video content in real-time without the long download times normally associated with these files. This technology does require the use of a special viewer called a "plug-in" which can usually be downloaded free of charge from the Internet. You can view an example of streaming audio and video content at the Haestad Methods Screening Room which can be accessed at:

Http://www.haestad.com/video/default.htm

A Web page is accessed using something called a Web browser, such as Netscape Navigator or Internet Explorer, which is launched locally from your desktop computer.

A host server – on your own network or an external Internet host – uploads contextual information to your client computer using the hypertext transfer protocol, or HTTP. Your Web browser software presents this information in an interactive, graphical fashion.

Within the browser window on your computer, you can jump to a hyper-linked page by clicking your mouse on an image or phrase that is mapped to another location using a unique address called the uniform resource locator, or URL. A URL allows users located anywhere in the world to access a directory and file located on a Web host server – also located anywhere in the world – from their personal computer by running a Web browser. In fact, a URL can address a file on your own hard drive or a file on your own network. Traditionally, files that a URL points to are blocks of ASCII text information that have been tagged using the hypertext markup language, known as HTML. This is the native format that is interpreted for display by Web browsers like Netscape Navigator or Internet Explorer. For example, the URL for the Haestad Methods home page is http://www.haestad.com (Figure 4-7).

In addition to serving up HTML formatted text, it is now possible to duplicate the functionality of more traditional applications using scripting languages which come in two flavors:

- Client-side

- Server-side.

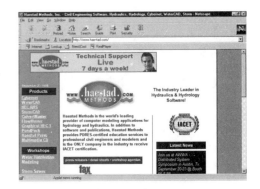

Figure 4-7: Haestad Methods homepage

Client-side languages like JavaScript and VBScript are interpreted and executed completely within the users browser while server-side languages such as Perl and TCL are executed first on the server and then the results are passed to the users browser using the Common Gateway Interface (CGI). Additionally, Sun Microsystem's Java allows clients to download and execute actual program code from Web servers.

While the Internet is the global network of inter-communicating servers that are linked together using a packet protocol, TCP/IP, there is also a private network equivalent called an Intranet. On the most basic level, an Intranet is simply an Internet that limits access to a closed group of people or resources. In other words, an Intranet uses the same communication protocols as the Internet, but access to this linked network is limited to a specific group of people. Technically an Intranet has the following characteristics:

- It uses open standards and protocols such as transmission control protocol/Internet protocol (TCP/IP), hypertext markup language (HTML), and simple mail transfer protocol (SMTP) to transfer information across the network.

- It is a closed system with limited access to the Internet so that the Internet at large is not able to reach the information contained on the Intranet.

- It usually uses web publishing, web databases, and HTML to share information, create documentation, and create shared workgroup applications.

The Intranet explosion arose when it became obvious that the same types of things you can do on the World Wide Web would be well-suited for managing internal corporate information, such as company policy, sales information and employee addresses.

Employees who want to learn about their company's health insurance policy or 401(K) plan, for instance, could simply use their computer to find the information on the Intranet.

Because Intranet content is generally proprietary and is either protected by passwords or maintained on an isolated network, companies don't have to worry about unauthorized people accessing the information.

Putting A Web Browser to Work for Your Company

Now that you've seen how the Web is so accessible, easy to use and powerful, it's time to share some ways that you can put the web to work for your company today. All you need is a Web browser, like Netscape Navigator or Microsoft Internet Explorer, and an Internet connection.

Locate Business and Product Information

Every Web browser maintains built-in links to free Web search engines. Using powerful services like Alta Vista, you can search for content on the Web just by typing in relevant keywords. Or you can use a search service like Yahoo that provides category-based searches. These index services organize information in content or subject hierarchies – much like a library.

New Web sites for construction and engineering are being posted every day. Good examples can be found at the AEC Info Center (Figure 4-8): **http://www.aecinfo.com**.

Figure 4-8: AEC Information Center

Find Projects and Clients

Civil Engineering consultants will want to visit Web sites maintained by state and federal agencies. Many agencies involved in high volume procurement of engineering services are realizing that the Web is a good place to publicize projects and advertise the need for services. That's because it allows them to maximize exposure and streamline the procurement process. Going to the Web saves money, so those who routinely work with federal and state agencies will find themselves getting more job leads from the Internet.

As a service to the civil engineering community, Haestad Methods recently launched **http://www.CivilProjects.com.** This site, containing RFP's and RFQ's is devoted to helping your company find the work it is looking for. For more detailed information on CivilProjects.com, read the article entitled "Using the Internet to find RFPs and RFQs."

Performing Technical Research

There is no limit to the amount of technical information available on the Web. However, because of the sheer volume, culling information that is actually useful can be challenging. In general, your best strategy is to maintain in your Web browser an assortment of links – sometimes known as "bookmarks" – to proven, productive data sources maintained by providers you know and trust. That way, you can easily revisit the sites – much like picking up a book where you left off.

A Web surfer is actually a data prospector – sifting through the raw Web content and mapping the paths to the most relevant information mines using the Web browser "favorites" or "bookmarks" feature. Experienced Web surfers are skilled at grading the quality of the content providers and can gauge a site's commitment to maintaining quality content over time.

Data mining is not random. It is a dynamic process that combines traditional use of search engines and diligent navigation of hypertext content jumps. In essence, the process requires a certain amount of mental focus because surfers will likely encounter an abundance of distractions along the way. It's easy for the neophyte – and even the skilled, for that matter – to be diverted by stumbling upon an interesting series of links and then drift completely out of the data hunt. If you

have the time, randomly jumping around can be entertaining and even educational. But surfing is an acquired skill, and because of the relative newness of the breakaway Internet phenomenon, there are still few masters.

For those in the engineering profession, colleges and universities offer some real Web gems that you will probably return to regularly. One good example is the civil engineering virtual library site maintained by Georgia Tech (Figure 4-9):

www.ce.gatech.edu/WWW-CE/home.html

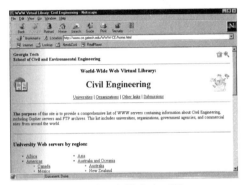

Figure 4-9: Georgia Tech virtual library

Obtain Software Support

The technical support experts from Haestad Methods are on the Internet frequently, downloading the newest printer drivers, updating libraries, and obtaining the latest software updates. Many of the most active pages are dedicated to providing end-user software support. The Internet is truly one of the best ways to obtain software assistance.

Users of our products frequently upload support files and send email queries to our software and engineering support staff. Most of our products now contain direct links to special support pages, which automatically inform the user if they have the most current version of our software

(Figure 4-10). These pages also provide access to our new searchable "knowledge base," (Figure 4-11) and a form to sign up for our electronic Water Distribution Modeling mailing list.

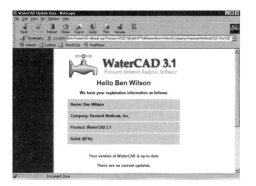

Figure 4-10: Updating software versions

Figure 4-11: Haestad Methods' knowledge base

Putting a Web Server to Work for Your Company

You've seen how pointing a web browser at the Internet can benefit your organization. However, you really can't achieve the greatest benefits until you stake out your own territory on the web.

Here we will share some ways that other civil engineering firms are using the Internet for active communication. Afterward, you will be ready to carry your company's message of service and success to the Internet.

Sharing Your Vision

If you're already using the Web, you probably realize that it holds valuable potential for marketing and gaining broad international exposure of your services. A corporate Web page is more than a billboard located along the information highway because, unlike a highway sign, you're not relying solely on random drive-by exposure. Rather, you expect interested people to deliberately track you down on the web, whether they know your specific address or simply search for you by keyword using a search engine.

Surfers will frequently come across a Web site when it is mentioned on another site about related services. By simply clicking the mouse button, they can then jump to the new site. These "virtual endorsements" of one site by another are highly prized because they can substantially increase a company's exposure.

For example, you can get to the Haestad Methods home page from many other home pages owned and operated by consulting firms, university professors, and agencies that use our products. Specialized industry sites that are operated by individuals or service organizations will add categorized links to your pages. A keyword search for "Haestad Methods" using Alta Vista reveals that the company's Web site is referenced by hundreds of Web locations.

Communicate and Transact with Clients

You can leverage Internet technology to enhance or extend your ability to communicate with project owners, architects and subcontractors. The Web is a universal pipeline that is replete with opportunities to extend its basic page-serving function. You can integrate database, email or ftp server technology into your Web site and actually deliver project-specific drawings, specifications and reports to contractors or owners.

Both Netscape and Microsoft have advanced standard binary protocols for extending Web functionality – plug-ins and ActiveX respectively. You can use Netscape compliant plug-ins; ActiveX client controls, or serve up documents recognized by ActiveX-enabled applications. These approaches let you display files that exist in other formats besides those implemented using the universal HTML format (e.g. Microsoft Word .doc files).

Clearly, using the web is faster and far less costly than using express mail, fax or long-distance phone service. Extended Web functionality enhances building a client communication framework that will streamline the way you do business.

Recruit New Employees

Many companies post employment opportunities on their Web sites. For professionals looking for a job, the Web is fertile ground.

One advantage of posting jobs on the Internet is that the prospect can often obtain a good feel for the company and its focus by browsing its full Web content. It also allows job prospects to prequalify themselves: if they don't like what they see on the Web, they're not likely to waste your time by applying for a job.

Building Your Web Page

To establish an organizational presence on the Web, you simply need to make a Web page available. How you do that depends on various considerations, including your objectives, available technical knowledge, computer resources, and budget.

For corporate Web sites, there are two hosting options available:

- **Virtual host.** Your Web page is hosted remotely by a company that specializes in providing this service. This is the least expensive approach, but there are limitations governing how you operate your page.

- **Local host.** Your Web page is hosted on your own Internet network server. While more expensive, this option gives you unlimited control over the operation on the site.

Service Provider

A connection to the Internet is the first item required. An Internet service provider, or ISP, can provide you with the physical connection to the Internet.

The first ISP that you deal with will probably provide one very important service for your company – registering your domain into the domain name system managed by Network Solutions at **http://rs.internic.net**. This name will serve as your unique Internet address. For example, Haestad Methods has reserved the name "haestad.com." For this right, you will pay a onetime registration fee of $70 for two years and no one else in the world can use that domain name for as long as the company continues to pay the annual $35 maintenance fee. The name you choose should be easy to remember and should be selected with care because it will serve as your Internet signpost for some time to come. A domain name is portable and can be carried from one ISP to another.

The Internet service provider business is quite competitive. Unlike cable or local telephone services, you might have a number of providers in your area offering a variety of billing and service packages.

Other services that your ISP can provide are email storing and forwarding and Usenet access. Many service providers offer virtual Web host services. Because this might be a valid option for your Web startup, you should be sure to discuss this with your potential service provider.

A list of Internet service providers can be found on the Web at **http://www.thelist.com**. Of course, if you don't have Internet access, you'll have to take a look in the yellow pages, or in the back of trade publications such as PC Week.

Bandwidth

Bandwidth is Internet jargon for the size of the information pipe. The larger the pipe, the faster your Web page data will move onto the Internet. The bandwidth you ultimately achieve will depend on the bandwidth the ISP can provide. A low-cost, but barely adequate, Web host could be run on a 28.8k modem connection. The ISP would provide you with a dedicated modem and number for your connection. Higher bandwidth connections are possible through the use of ISDN (64k to 128k), Frame Relay (56k to 1.54mbps), or leased lines (56k to 45mbps).

Bandwidth is Internet jargon for the size of the information pipe. The larger the pipe, the faster your Web page data will move onto the Internet.

Find out how much bandwidth your ISP can offer. This will affect your ability to effectively handle the growing crowd of visitors who will flock to your Web site as you introduce new content or capabilities.

The question of available ISP bandwidth becomes even more crucial as you contemplate higher connection speed. With a 28.8k modem connection, your server's modem is the bottleneck and ISP bandwidth is not an issue. This will not be the case if you run at 45mbps. So connection speed might dictate whether to use a local provider or seek a large regional provider with many high-speed connection points to the Internet.

Virtual Hosting

For starters, especially if you go with a 28.8k modem connection, you might want to consider using your ISP's virtual host services. This way, visitors to your page will not be put off by slow server response time. Web surfers are becoming less tolerant of pages that load slowly, and if it takes too long, they will simply "hang up" on you, much like a telephone customer left on hold too long.

Even on a virtual host, you will write the content and organize your Web page. The essential difference is that you will upload the Web page files to the virtual host. But, from a Web visitor's point of view, that's transparent.

The cost of virtual Web hosting varies from one provider to the next. In general, you can expect to pay anywhere from $25 to $99 per month depending on the amount of storage space allotted and data transferred monthly. Make sure that the ISP explains any limitations that may apply concerning access limits and allowable Web space – which could increase your fees or prevent you from expanding your Web site.

Web Content

Remember that the Web is about publishing. Most of the content that will find it's way into the company's maiden page is very likely residing on a hard drive somewhere in the organization right this minute. If you publish corporate brochures, churn out Standard Form 254/255s or prepare formal proposals, you probably have a wealth of raw content at hand. If it already exists in desktop publishing or word processing format, you are very close. Setting up your Web then becomes a process of reformatting the text and images into a hyper-media presentation using HTML.

A host of tools are available for creating HTML – Microsoft FrontPage and Macromedia DreamWeaver are two commonly used products. These tools provide WYSIWYG editing which allows page editing in an environment that graphically displays the content in the same format that it will appear in an actual Web browser – what you and your visitors will see. This is great for beginners since they are not forced to memorize HTML control tags.

As the Web authors gain more skill and knowledge, they frequently forgo the WYSIWYG style editors and use native HTML tags for formatting. This gives the Web author greater control over page appearance. In fact, the Haestad Methods Webmaster edits entirely with HTML tags in an ASCII text editor.

Local Server

If your organization chooses to run a local Web server, you will need server software. The two major players in the computer platform arena on the Internet are Unix and Windows NT.

Haestad Methods runs a dedicated Windows NT server. Most of our clients will be taking the same approach, simply because the vast majority of our users are running Windows or DOS applications on PCs.

Many commercial and freeware products are available for a variety of computer platforms. Microsoft has just released Internet Information Server 4.0, a Web server package (Apache HTTP Server is a free Web server for the Unix platform).

The cost to locally host a site depends on the choices you make for the hardware, software, and connection speed. Of course, most cost estimates don't include the cost of time and effort associated with maintaining a Web presence. Someone in the organization must act as Webmaster – the individual who has primary responsibility for maintaining and updating the site.

And in Conclusion

In this article, a great deal of time was spent introducing technical concepts and examining costs associated with startup and operation. In a way, the transition to the Web is akin to the adoption of CAD by engineering organizations.

With CAD, initially a lot of energy was spent looking at startup costs, selecting and comparing alternatives, and overcoming skepticism. Eventually, management came to the realization that the manpower costs of the technicians and engineers using the system (and their training) eclipsed costs of these issues. These true costs are offset by the productivity gains realized by the organization.

As the World Wide Web becomes a standard component of your company's communication infrastructure, you will discover that the collection, authoring, organization and presentation of the content of your Web site are where the true costs are. You will also find that the more adept you get at producing this content and exploiting Internet technology, the more productive your company will become.

And just like with CAD, there were early adopters and late adopters of the technology. All had different experiences and some achieved more reward than others. Will your organization be an early adopter or a late adopter of the Internet technology? It's almost too late to decide.

Due to its importance to the Civil Engineering industry, this article has been reprinted (with updates) from Haestad Press's 1997 Practical Guide to Hydraulics and Hydrology.

Editor: Jeremy Haynes

Using the Internet to Find RFPs and RFQs

Reel in dollars for your firm by searching for Requests For Proposals (RFPs) and Requests For Qualifications (RFQs) on the Internet.

Using the Internet effectively to find RFPs and RFQs is simply a matter of knowing where and how to look. Thousands of local and international publications, government agencies and civil engineering interest groups maintain areas on their websites where RFPs and RFQs are posted on a regular basis. Once you have taken the time to locate and familiarize yourself with these sites, you will finally be able to focus your energy on creating proposals rather than searching for requests.

Generate a list of RFP sources

Jot down the places you normally look when searching for RFPs and RFQs – newspaper and magazine classified ads, public and private organization newsletters, clipping services, etc. See whether or not a website exists for each source and if it does, find out the URL. If you can not find this information directly from the source, call the customer service line or conduct an Internet search using a search engine such as Yahoo! or AltaVista (Figure 4-12).

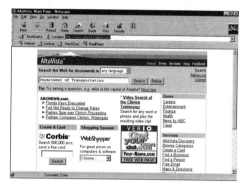

Figure 4-12: AltaVista search engine

Use Your Favorite WWW Search Engine to Find New Sites

Run queries on newspapers, government agencies and civil engineering businesses in your town or state and follow links from your favorite civil engineering related webpages to find new RFP and RFQ sources. Other great sources for finding

RFPs and RFQs on the Internet are sites like Haestad Methods "CivilProjects" and Pollution Online's "RFPs/Projects for Bid Search" which allow you to search through thousands of RFP and RFQ advertisements.

Spend Time Navigating Your Way Around Each Site

On some sites it's tricky to find RFPs and RFQs. Since each site is organized differently, it is important to be patient and take your time when browsing. If you find yourself having trouble, email or call the host and ask where to find the RFP and RFQ listings. This is especially important to remember when dealing with municipalities that

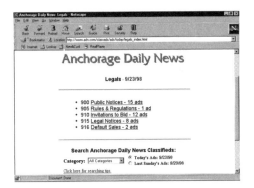

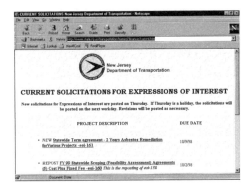

Figure 4-13: Newspaper homepages

can post RFPs and RFQs under anything from "What's New?" to "Opportunities." Newspapers, on the other hand, are a bit easier to navigate (Figure 4-13). On most sites, you can jump right to the classified section from the home page. From there you can search or browse the appropriate section (usually, legal or public notices). Search words like "engineer", "design", "bid" and "proposal" yield the best results. Some newspapers will even email the results of your customized searches to you on a daily or weekly basis.

Create Links to RFP and RFQ Sites From Your Desktop

Once you have found the area where RFPs and RFQs are posted and have spent enough time browsing to tell whether or not the site is up-to-date and well-maintained, create a shortcut from your desktop to the site. This can also be done with the bookmark feature on your web browser.

Check and Update Links to Your RFP and RFQ Sites Regularly

Obviously, publications are updated depending on frequency of circulation. Checking newspaper sites on Sundays and Thursdays should be plenty. However, the vast majority of organizations update their websites weekly so it's best to spend a small amount of time each week checking all your links for new RFP and RFQ listings. Finally, remember to keep your list up-to-date by changing site addresses in your link whenever a URL changes and deleting sites that continually do not turn up good leads.

What Is CivilProjects.com?

CivilProjects (Figure 4-14), an Internet site created and maintained by Haestad Methods, serves the civil engineering community by providing an efficient, effective, and easy way to search for current RFPs and RFQs throughout the world. New and upcoming solicitations for engineering services from public and private organizations are added daily and expired postings removed so that CivilProjects always remains up-to-date. Additionally, CivilProjects contains links to a variety of other civil engineering related websites to keep consultants abreast of the latest professional and educational opportunities and news.

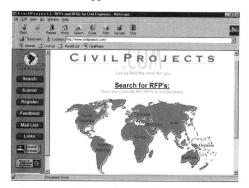

Figure 4-14: http://www.CivilProjects.com

CivilProjects boasts a no-nonsense interface that allows easy navigation through each area of the site. Visitors are never more than a few clicks away from finding an RFP or RFQ in their area, connecting to our "Link of the Week", learning about the latest courses offered for CEUs, sharing thoughts on CivilProjects with Haestad Methods or even submitting an RFP or RFQ to the site themselves.

Searching for RFPs and RFQs

Both the "Search" button to the left of the page and icon to the right connect you to the CivilProjects RFP/RFQ database. Here civil engineers can find, list, and print out consulting opportunities by running queries on a keyword, state, or country.

Using the keyword search option allows consultants to locate projects based on words or phrases that frequently appear in RFPs and RFQs of interest to them. For instance, submitting a keyword query on "wastewater" automatically connects users to a detailed list of all the RFPs and RFQs in the CivilProjects database containing that search word, regardless of geographical location.

Conversely, searching by state or country yields a list of RFPs and RFQs related only in terms of location. This allows users to browse all of the projects open for bid in a specific area. A state or country search is not only an effective way to connect consultants to job opportunities but also to provide information about other civil engineering projects going on around them.

Lists compiled using any one of the three search methods are organized in the same fashion. CivilProjects displays RFPs and RFQs in ascending order of closing date or response deadline. Furthermore, as a refreshing alternative to the compacted formats of newspaper and magazine RFP and RFQ classified listings, all information in the CivilProjects database is conveniently broken down and arranged by category – project description, organization name, contact, qualifications, estimated amount, etc.

Submitting an RFP or RFQ

RFPs and RFQs can be submitted to the CivilProjects site by selecting either the "Submit" button to the left or the icon to the right. After filling out and submitting the online form, Haestad Methods reviews the information and posts the RFP or RFQ to CivilProjects within a week.

Registering as a CivilProjects User

Registering as a CivilProjects user initiates two way communication – mediated by Haestad Methods – between organizations soliciting engineering services and the consulting civil engineers seeking these opportunities. Filling out the online registration form under either the "Register" button or icon allows Haestad Methods to automatically email members with information about current and upcoming projects in their area as new RFPs and RFQs are posted to the CivilProjects site.

Contacting Haestad Methods

Visitors to the CivilProjects site can conveniently email their comments, suggestions, and questions to Haestad Methods via the "Feedback" link. Since this submission form requires the entry of an email address, users will always receive a response from Haestad Methods.

The CivilProjects Mailing List

Under this link, visitors may either subscribe or unsubscribe to the CivilProjects mailing list. This service exists simply to notify users via email of the latest updates, additions and modifications to the CivilProjects site.

World Wide Web Links

Clicking on the "Links" button brings visitors to the CivilProjects "Link of the Week" as well as our Business or Educational Opportunities directory which include links to sites such as the American Society of Civil Engineers (ASCE), Public Works Online and the Air Force Institute of Technology. Haestad Methods updates these links regularly and visitors are invited to submit suggestions for additions to these pages.

Author: Kelly L'Heureux

References

Haestad Press. 1997. *Practical Guide to Hydraulics and Hydrology.* Waterbury, CT: Haestad Press.

Index

Notes

Notes

Notes

Notes